Guidance for Librarians Transitioning to a New Environment

Guidance for Librarians Transitioning to a New Environment offers practical advice for those hoping to transition into a different type or size of institution. Written by librarians who have successfully navigated such changes, the book encourages consideration of unexplored opportunities.

Drawing on the authors' own experiences, as well as surveys and interviews conducted with those working in different types of libraries, the book will provide librarians with a field guide for surviving and thriving in their new environment. It will do so by making suggestions for how librarians can orient themselves to their new library, add context to their CV or résumé, get started with presenting and publishing, and manage culture shock and emotions. Each chapter will also provide the opportunity for the librarian to reflect on relevant aspects of their own situation and move forward with the help of action items.

Guidance for Librarians Transitioning to a New Environment is essential reading for librarians who are considering or in the process of making a career move, as well as those working on career planning. The book will also be helpful for library science school faculty and career counselors who are advising current students and library managers who want to help their new hires transition in the most effective way.

Tina Herman Buck is the Electronic Resources Librarian at the University of Central Florida. She has worked in public libraries of widely varying sizes, a multi-type library cooperative, a very small university, and a very large one, all in the United States. All her jobs have been in technical services, with varying percentages of public services mixed in.

Sara Duff is the Acquisitions and Collection Assessment librarian at the University of Central Florida. Before that, she worked for seven years as a librarian at Gulf Coast State College. Though she focuses in acquisitions now, she's done quite a bit of public services work at the community college level.

Routledge Guides to Practice in Libraries, Archives and Information Science

Guidance for Librarians Transitioning to a New Environment
Tina Herman Buck and Sara Duff

For more information about this series, please visit: www.routledge.com/Routledge-Guides-to-Practice-in-Libraries-Archives-and-Information-Science/book-series/RGPLAIS

Guidance for Librarians Transitioning to a New Environment

Tina Herman Buck and Sara Duff

LONDON AND NEW YORK

First published 2021
by Routledge
2 Park Square, Milton Park, Abingdon, Oxon OX14 4RN

and by Routledge
52 Vanderbilt Avenue, New York, NY 10017

Routledge is an imprint of the Taylor & Francis Group, an informa business

© 2021 Tina Herman Buck and Sara Duff

The right of Tina Herman Buck and Sara Duff to be identified as authors of this work has been asserted by them in accordance with sections 77 and 78 of the Copyright, Designs and Patents Act 1988.

All rights reserved. No part of this book may be reprinted or reproduced or utilised in any form or by any electronic, mechanical, or other means, now known or hereafter invented, including photocopying and recording, or in any information storage or retrieval system, without permission in writing from the publishers.

Trademark notice: Product or corporate names may be trademarks or registered trademarks, and are used only for identification and explanation without intent to infringe.

British Library Cataloguing-in-Publication Data
A catalogue record for this book is available from the British Library

Library of Congress Cataloging-in-Publication Data
A catalog record has been requested for this book

ISBN: 978-0-367-19903-6 (hbk)
ISBN: 978-0-367-19906-7 (pbk)
ISBN: 978-0-429-24399-8 (ebk)

Typeset in Times New Roman
by Newgen Publishing UK

Contents

	Preface	vii
	Acknowledgements	xi
	Glossary and abbreviations	xii
	List of librarians interviewed	xiv
1	A new size or type of library	1
2	Exploring new opportunities	25
3	Preparing for interviews and promotion	34
4	Mentorship	61
5	Being the new person	74
6	Looking inward: managing your emotions	88
7	Publishing, presenting, and conferencing	103
8	Tying it all together	117
	Appendix A: Survey on librarian career path and attitudes	131
	Appendix B: Example résumé and CV	137
	Index	150

Preface

Both authors have gone through significant library transitions, moving between types and sizes of libraries. We both realized independently that there is very little information or advice on the market for librarians who want to make this kind of big change effectively and efficiently. We started talking to each other about this topic in the midst of Sara's transition to the University of Central Florida and realized that if we had these experiences and frustrations, surely others would as well. We thought of what we wish people had told us before we switched, and new things we tried that worked, and decided to put them all together in this book. But it wasn't enough to lean only on our experiences. We wanted to make sure we weren't isolated cases, so we put out a call on email lists and message boards in various countries. In the end, we interviewed 23 librarians who have worked in a wide variety of library environments and wove quotes from those interviews throughout this book, credited to those librarians.

As we began writing the book and talking to librarians, there was a near universal response. Virtually everyone we spoke to said something to the effect of, "I'm so glad you're writing this!" People echoed our view that this has been a gap in the library literature, and that they themselves had wished for something like this.

This book is taken from our experiences and research. Our goal has been to offer support and encouragement for librarians in transition but not everything on offer here will work for every situation a librarian might find themselves in. We encourage you to consider everything in the book, bypass those strategies that aren't appealing or applicable to your situation, and partake of what is helpful to you. Please take from this wide array of ideas and advice as it suits you, with our best wishes for your success.

Before delving further, we would like to tell you our individual stories and why we wanted to write this book.

Sara's story

I am the Acquisitions & Collection Assessment Librarian at the University of Central Florida. If you had told me eight years ago that I would end up at one of the largest research universities in the United States, I would not have believed it to be possible.

My first library conference was in the spring of 2009. I was a graduate student, full of energy and ideas, but didn't yet know where I would fit in the library profession. This was during the "Great Recession," and finding a job was a pressing, seemingly impossible, issue. Almost every big school or library system had hiring freezes in place, and with no end yet in sight, people were tense.

With all this in mind, I went to a session about finding a library job. On the panel were library representatives from different types of libraries, including a large research university and a county-wide public library system. The room was packed, all seats were filled and people were standing in clumps around the perimeter. The discussion went on for a while, covering many aspects of the library job search, but the point that stood out to me the most then, and that I remember most clearly now, was about moving between library types. The representative from the research university library told the standing-room-only crowd in no uncertain terms that the type of library you started at would be the type of library you worked in for the rest of your career. He conceded that yes, some skills transfer, but that academic and public libraries were so different that his university never hired people from other library types. The public library representative then agreed with him! The exception, they both stated, was community college librarians. They got a taste of working with the public but still did academic librarian work, so therefore community college librarians alone could transfer between library types throughout their career. Hands shot up from mid-career librarians around the room and some heated discussion ensued, but the authorities at the front of the room did not budge.

So, not really knowing where I wanted to spend the rest my of career, I looked for a job at a community college library. It worked out very well for me but not in the ways the panelists assumed. It wasn't the unique blend of working with the public and doing academic work that made me eligible to work at a research university, it was the experience I gained working at a small library where the librarians all did a little bit of everything. I got to teach library instruction classes, become embedded in online classes, do in-person and online reference, run outreach events, and, in what became my career focus, work in technical services. Because all of these different aspects of librarianship were a part of my job, I got to see pretty quickly which aspects I loved and which ones didn't come naturally to me. I think this is true for all small libraries, regardless of type. When you have a small team, everyone has a hand in everything.

Throughout my years working as a librarian, I discovered that what the panelists had said was not really true. I know many people, including people from the panelist's research library, who have worked in multiple types of libraries without issue. Yet, this myth is persistent. When I began to prepare for my new job at a research university library, a lot of people expressed surprise and wondered how the transition would go. "Oh wow, that's going to be very different!" I heard again and again. And yes, it was quite different, but ultimately I was able to figure out how to scale up my work and have settled in quite well. I want this book to empower those who want to make the leap to go for it, to be able to avoid some of the pitfalls I noticed, and to know that they aren't alone in trying to make such a change.

Tina's story

I started my career as the head of technical services in a small town library, serving a community of about 30,000. More than 20 years later, I'm the electronic resources librarian at one of the largest universities in the country: University of Central Florida (UCF), which had over 66,000 students enrolled in the fall of 2017 (www.ucf.edu/about-ucf/facts/). In between, I worked at a 28-branch county-wide public library system; a small private university with an enrollment under 5,000; and a library cooperative that provided services to libraries of all types, plus stops in two different city library systems.

There's a lot of variation between those libraries but there's a solid core of similarities, too. Each new position required learning: the job, the community, the local lingo. But I was always able to build on what came before. Everything I've learned has been useful as I've moved along, regardless of where I learned it. Different types and sizes of libraries have far more in common than some might think.

I've encountered some prejudices toward "the other" that I hope to help dispel with this book: Academic librarians who seemed to think that public librarians don't deal with any level of complexity in their work and function at a routine, uncomplicated level. Public librarians who seemed to think that academic librarians have it easy because they're not dealing with "the public." In all cases, it's been painful to hear these disparaging generalities about fellow librarians and surprising at how strongly held those opinions were.

In my most recent job search, I was looking for a new challenge, something different than the job I had held for the past nine years. Either academic or public was fine by me; I would choose based on the appeal of the location, the connection I felt with the people I interviewed with, and whether the job itself sounded challenging, interesting, and full of potential for growth.

I remember a phone interview with a large city library system. The interviewers sounded dubious that I could transition to working in an urban library, even though I had worked in the downtown libraries of two other city systems. They seemed to think that someone working at a private university was very sheltered and – I don't really know – only dealt with genteel, erudite scholars in hushed, stately rooms. I tried to explain my downtown library experiences and that my private university library interacted with plenty of challenging people from the broader community: a main thoroughfare and bus stop were less than a block away and we weren't in a ritzy area. But those facts were rejected. I was at a private university and therefore couldn't possibly transition to a public.

I had another phone interview with an exclusive large academic research library. It was clear from the start that my "varied" background was a huge stumbling block. They wanted someone coming from another research library. I was an outsider and I couldn't possibly understand.

This isn't to say that I was the perfect candidate for either of those jobs. But my background, in a variety of types and sizes of libraries, was a problem. It shouldn't have been. Knowledge, skills, abilities, and attitudes are to be questioned and probed in a job interview. But not a background in other types and sizes. You can learn, grow, contribute, build, and synthesize wherever you are and wherever you go.

Not everyone encounters such prejudicial attitudes and many librarians are warmly welcoming of colleagues from a variety of backgrounds. But there are differences between types and sizes of libraries that Sara and I both wish we had known before making our various transitions. The information wouldn't have kept us from making those moves but it would have made the process easier. After all, less time getting up to speed means more time accomplishing the library work we value so much.

Acknowledgements

We would like to thank our interviewees who shared generously of their time and insights. None of you seemed to think you were amazing, but we were humbled and astounded by each of you. We also must thank those who helped distribute our survey, those who responded to the survey, and those who volunteered for interviews. It wasn't easy choosing who to interview and we know we left excellent candidates behind due simply to our time constraints.

We also want to thank our colleagues at the University of Central Florida, especially Ying Zhang, Athena Hoeppner, and Sarah Norris. At UCF, we've encountered as friendly, supportive, and highly competent a group of colleagues as any librarian could hope for. Go Knights!

Finally, we want to extend appreciation for our mentors and former colleagues who helped shape us into the librarians we are today, and for our editorial team at Routledge for providing us the opportunity to write this book.

Glossary and abbreviations

ACRL | Association of College and Research Libraries.
ALA | American Library Association. This is a professional organization for librarians and library staff headquartered in Chicago, Illinois. It has several subdivisions in library specialized areas, and many of those have committees made up of member librarians. ALA holds a large annual conference each year in the United States.
CEO | Chief Executive Officer. Though most will be familiar with this term in the business realm, in Canada public libraries are run by a CEO who is typically an experienced librarian. This is roughly equivalent to the library director position in the United States.
Charleston | This refers to the conference formally called "Charleston Conference: Issues in Serial and Book Acquisition." It takes places in Charleston, South Carolina every fall, and is an important conference for acquisitions librarians.
Community colleges | A two-year degree-granting educational organization. Some may now offer select four-year degrees, but the bulk of the programs will be designed for students to transfer to a university to complete their bachelor's degree.
DRM | Digital Rights Management: restrictions on use of digital media (such as eBooks)
ERM | Electronic resource management. Sometimes ERMs: electronic resources management system. Sometimes a part of the ILS, sometimes a standalone system.
FAME | Florida Association for Media in Education. This is a professional organization for school librarians and media specialists in Florida.

Glossary and abbreviations xiii

FLA	Florida Library Association. Since Tina and Sara are currently located in Florida, they refer to the Florida Library Association. However, most states have their own library organization with a similar name.
IFLA	International Federation of Library Associations and Institutions. A worldwide organization representing the interests of library services and users.
ILS	Integrated Library System. Sometimes called an LMS, or Library Management System, or LSP, Library Services Platform. This is the software that libraries use to catalog, circulate, and track acquisitions of library materials.
MLIS	Master of Library and Information Studies. Sometimes called Master of Library and Information Science, or MLS for Master of Library Science. Though there are multiple names, the degrees are essentially the same. This is typically the degree required for a professional librarian in the United States and Canada.
Multi-type Library Organization	Also known as a multi-type library co-operative. This organization will offer local training to a set of all types of libraries within a set geographic area. The organization may do group licensing or handle specific task for the group like Interlibrary Loan.
PLA	Public Library Association.
SLA	Special Library Association.
State Library	In the United States, most states have a State Library that handles library business for the entire state. It is run by the state government and will typically have a State Librarian. The State Library may do things like offer free trainings for all librarians in the state or a group licensing opportunity.
UCF	University of Central Florida, where both authors currently work.

Librarians interviewed

Andy McDonald is a library manager in the UK who has worked in both public and academic libraries.

Anna Semmens is in library administration in the UK and has worked in many types of libraries in the UK, including school libraries, public libraries, and academic libraries, and at a public library in New Zealand.

Audrey Snowden is a public librarian in the US who has previously worked at a school library in Mexico and in school libraries and public libraries of varying sizes in the US.

Brian Johnson* is an academic librarian in the US who previously worked at a state library.

Deb Silverman is a librarian who has worked at a law library, public library, academic library, health sciences library, and at vendors, in the US and Canada.

Diane Van Gorden is a school librarian in the rural US.

Fred Gitner is in library administration at a public library and has also worked in special libraries in the US.

Jenn Jones is a public library CEO in Canada who has worked in academic libraries and public libraries of various sizes.

Jinnie Trabulsi is a children's librarian in the US who has worked in public and academic libraries.

Jodie Delgado is a public library CEO in Canada and has previously worked in school libraries and public libraries in the US.

Kady Ferris is a public librarian who previously worked in academic libraries in the US.

Kat Kan is a public librarian and bibliographic specialist for a vendor who previously worked in school and academic libraries in the US.

Librarians interviewed xv

Kathy Webb is an academic library director in the US who has also worked in public libraries.

Lisa Samchuk is an instructor in a library technician program in Canada, who has previously worked in academic libraries.

Marian Royal is a public library director in the US, and has also worked in hospital libraries, academic health sciences libraries, and school libraries.

Maureen Penn is a public library CEO in Canada, who has previously worked for public libraries of various sizes and a library vendor in Canada.

Pam Bidwell is a library school senior lecturer at university in New Zealand and has previously worked in a public library in the UK, academic libraries in Australia and New Zealand, and as a library school lecturer in Fiji and Palau.

Ronit Barenboim is a librarian at a law firm in Canada who has previously worked in academic libraries and at a library vendor.

Shelly Grace is the director of a multi-type library organization and has previously worked in corporate and academic libraries.

Sonia Smith is an academic law librarian in Canada and previously worked as a children's librarian and academic librarian in Canada, and as an academic librarian in Mexico.

Stewart Donovan* is a librarian at a special library who has also worked in academic, corporate, and public libraries in the US.

Yolanda Hood is an academic librarian in the US who has worked in academic libraries of various sizes in the US and at a small academic library in Canada.

Yolande Wilburn is a director at a public library in the US and has previously worked in various levels of academic libraries and public libraries in both urban and rural environments in the US.

*Pseudonyms provided at the request of the librarians interviewed.

1 A new size or type of library

There are many reasons why librarians might decide to take a job at a drastically different library. However, the transition is not always straightforward. Librarians should consider the challenges they could face before they make the transition to a different size or type of library, so that they will be better prepared. Though many librarians have moved between types and sizes, the authors had previously heard a widespread myth that librarians are pigeonholed into one library type throughout their career. A survey demonstrates that there are differences in attitudes toward moving between type and size depending on the answerer's own career path. This chapter includes a discussion of similarities and differences between types of libraries, including patron focus, philosophies of library activities, and types of services and classes offered. This chapter suggests other options such as temporary or contract positions, rural libraries, and working in developing countries. There is a discussion of misconceptions about different library jobs. This chapter also has advice from interviewees who have changed library environment.

Some librarians have a career plan in mind from the start and steadily work toward their goals, adjusting as needed but always with a larger plan in mind. Some simply want to be working librarians and only consider the next step when something, internal or external, causes the realization that the current situation isn't quite right.

Tina falls squarely in the latter camp. It is only looking back over a long and varied career that she sees how she came to feel qualified to write a book of support and guidance for librarians considering a change in library environment. At each step along the way, she had little awareness that changes between large and small libraries or public and academic (or public to private or across various geographic areas, for that matter) were particularly significant moves, ones that might cause a more planful librarian to proceed with caution.

We can guess that you picked up this book because you're curious about the potential of transitioning to another library environment. Perhaps you're a career planner and are looking for input. You might have a sense that it's time to move on from your current position. Maybe you're out of work or are at the very beginning of your library career and want help getting a job. In any of these circumstances, your first thought may be to stay within the type and/ or size library that you are most familiar with, whether due to experience on the job or as a patron. The authors want to show you that a broader world of opportunity is available to you. (While the focus of this book is on changing library environments, there is also plenty to consider for those making any job change.) We suspect that that some librarians haven't considered these options due to lack of information, preconceived notions, or having no colleagues who have made such a change. Some librarians have encountered bias against changing type – an attitude that fortunately seems to be fading over time – and may be leery as a result.

Thus, we'll begin with a look at Tina's real-life job transitions as a sort of case study about changing library environments. As an entry point to the rest of this book, we'll focus on the aspects that are most relevant to our content: the appeal of a particular job and its environment, positives and negatives, and then the reason(s) Tina moved on.

After that, we'll move into a discussion of why a librarian should consider such a change and look at some differences and similarities between types and sizes. We'll offer some options that you may not have considered for your career. From there, we'll dig into misconceptions that may be holding people back. Then we'll see the results of the authors' survey (Duff & Buck, 2019) of librarian perceptions of moving to a different environment. Finally, we'll gain some insights from our interviewees who have changed types or sizes.

During college and graduate school, Tina worked as a para-professional in the public library system, first as a shelver in the children's department and then in the catalog department doing a variety of copy cataloging tasks. It was a city system with about 20 branches. In the catalog department, taught and mentored by the professional catalogers, Tina found work that she was fascinated by and that prompted her to begin the Master of Library Science (MLS) program at the local university, focusing on cataloging and related coursework. Her stint in the children's room instilled a lifelong fondness for picture books, but in terms of career expectations, Tina was sure she would become a cataloger in a public library and would always be one. Some of her fellow MLS students were planning to work at academic libraries, prison libraries, or other environments. The catalogers, archivists, reference and children's librarians, and the management types seem to already have self-selected and it didn't occur to Tina that her intended path would ever change, in terms of either library type or job duties.

That changed a bit when she landed her first professional job as a technical services librarian in a single-site small-town library. The appeal of the job was primarily the giddy delight of landing that first professional position in her desired sector of librarianship. The location was a positive, providing the opportunity to move to an area where she knew people. The job advertisement seemed like a good fit though the technical services components were broader than purely cataloging. Of course, the venue was a public library; at that stage it probably wouldn't have occurred to Tina to apply to another type. Once she started the position, her adjustments included being the only technical services professional in the building, doing reference shifts (having taken little reference coursework in school), participating in collection development (having taken no collection-related coursework), being part of two library consortia, managing staff, and being recognized as the "library lady" everywhere she went in her new hometown. She learned about processing a wide variety of materials, small town politics, and the ILS (integrated library system, which was managed by the consortia central site), including her first system migration.

After a few years, Tina realized she would have to move to a larger library in order to do higher-level cataloging. The small-town library didn't have OCLC, a widely used cataloging utility; original and complex copy cataloging needs were turned over to the consortia that managed the regional ILS. So, in pursuit of expanded professional responsibilities and skill-building, Tina became the assistant head of technical services in a nearby city with a public library system of eight or nine branches. She was still solely aware of the public library realm. The change in library size permitted her to get that experience doing complex cataloging on OCLC. She also got the opportunity to assist in managing a larger, more complicated technical services department and to work with professional cataloger colleagues. However, the larger library also had a much greater need for staffing at the multiple reference desks. Reference hours were part of Tina's duties and staffing shortages kept her on the reference desk for a significant portion of the workweek, impacting what she could accomplish in technical services. Thus, when a colleague mentioned an opening for a technical services consultant at a multi-type library cooperative, Tina was faced with her first potential move across types.

The multi-type cooperative provided training, auxiliary collections, cooperative purchasing, interlibrary loan, and numerous other supports for their hundred-plus member libraries across the region. Tina had taken continuing education classes from the librarians at the multi-type so had some familiarity with the institution. The job sounded interesting, but she worried that not working in a more conventional library would be a career dead-end.

Remembering this misguided concern many years later, Tina can only shake her head because that job became one of the biggest growth periods of her career. It also led to numerous long-term, positive professional connections. Skills and knowledge built during this job opened the door to many opportunities. These include: volunteering to vanguard the adoption of a new ILS acquisitions module and to train other institutions on it set Tina up for work in the ILS migrations that happened in most of her subsequent institutions; co-managing a statewide materials purchasing cooperative set her up to understand purchasing rules, vendor processing, and acquisitions complexities; conducting frequent training sessions for librarians and library staff provided evidence of her capacity for performing library instruction when she applied to her first academic library. The job at the multi-type cooperative also finely honed her sense of the importance of being open to learning new skills and trying new things, even if you must figure things out for yourself and fail occasionally along the way.

In terms of the number of librarians and staff, the multi-type was essentially staffed at the same level as a small library, with about seven librarians and 15 staff. But Tina's world of professional associates expanded greatly. While she was the only technical services librarian at the multi-type, that gap was filled by committee work for the ILS consortia with other member libraries and by connections to her peers at similar multi-types across the state. As part of her job as technical services consultant, she interacted with librarians from a wide range of libraries: different types (such as hospitals, schools, specials, and local history centers, in addition to the publics and academics); geographic realities from urban to rural; and patron size from populous to tiny. The libraries also varied greatly in their funding, local support, and staffing levels. None of these factors seemed to have any relationship to the creativity, dedication, or quality of service demonstrated by the librarian. In hindsight, Tina can see where the seeds of this book might have been sown during this time.

Tina reluctantly left the multi-type when family needs took her halfway across the country. Her primary motivation in her job search was simply to find a job quickly but she did reject an early offer of part-time cataloging work at a university. Library type played no part in her rejection; the part-time hours, very low pay, and long commute were the major negative factors. Instead, she found a full-time position with a strong collection management component at a large countywide public system with nearly 30 branches. Tina's area was primarily print serials and standing orders and, lacking a very strong background in these, she was surprised to get the job. Looking back, she can see that her broad-based experience was probably her appeal. With cataloging know-how, she could help with the backlog of standing order cataloging; she knew some acquisitions, procurement, and collection management; had worked in a couple of public systems with multiple branches; had some experience with changing ILSs; was comfortable communicating with people across an institution, regardless of rank or role; and had been a supervisor in every job. Each of these elements was a component of her new job. The fact that she, as a recent transplant to the area, was able to start almost immediately was probably attractive too.

The new job made Tina part of a well-oiled, highly competent collection management team. It was a well-funded system with a strong focus on providing excellent library services to their population. She learned a lot and certainly had more to learn about collection management at that level, but after a relatively short tenure, her husband's job took them halfway across the country again.

She quickly found a job as a cataloger at the public library in her new city, a system with about 20 locations. This was the kind of job she had envisioned herself in during library school. The city system was similar in scope to the one she worked at during library school and the scope of the job as a full-time cataloger was her original goal. Ironically, she found that wasn't what she wanted. The catalogers and cataloging staff were assigned very specific areas and Tina found herself cataloging non-fiction DVDs all day long. The department required every detail on the DVD case to be in the bibliographic record, with no leeway for a cataloger's judgment of important versus marginal information. Tina found it frustrating to spend what she considered to be unnecessary time on each title when there was a considerable cataloging backlog – many book-trucks of materials were unavailable to the public. It was the first time that she felt bored by cataloging – or perhaps it's more accurate to say that she was bored by only cataloging and according to chafing rules.

The library was getting ready for an ILS migration and Tina got herself on the migration team, representing cataloging and related interests. She doesn't recall exactly how this came to be, but likely her experience with and interest in these projects were strongly contributing factors. Soon she was sitting in on meetings with the vendor team and learning more about the guts of ILS systems than she ever had before. She was also drafted to work with IT personnel on improvements to the public online catalog and to create training documentation for the cataloging staff. These duties alleviated the boredom somewhat, but the basic frustration remained.

So, when a technical services librarian position at a small university in town became available, Tina was intrigued. The job advertisement suggested a lot of variety – something she now recognized as important to her sense of satisfaction – including acquisitions, cataloging, the ILS and public catalog, reference, and instruction. While the venue was obviously a different type of library, Tina keyed in on the similarities between the job posting and her own experience, rather than the change of type. After a lengthy interview process, she was offered the job and became an academic librarian. Having worked in numerous environments, moving to a one-building library with a small staff didn't seem like that big a change, on the face of it.

Learning how a university was organized was an early challenge. Tina made sense of it by relating the different colleges and departments to public library branches, each having unique elements as well as commonalities. Discussion of curricular committees, faculty senate, and similar academic terminology was unfamiliar and a bit disorienting, but such matters remained on the edges of her awareness.

On the other hand, cataloging, acquisitions, and processing were familiar, and new areas in technical services were exciting to explore. Tina implemented ILS functionality that had lain dormant since a migration the previous year, which yielded opportunities for her to learn the administration of the system. Her colleague in technical services, the electronic resources and serials librarian, shared lessons in management of academic electronic resources, a growing area that Tina had little experience with.

Public services were different from what she had known. Providing reference service in academia was strange for one so accustomed to the public library mantra of "find the answer for the patron." Tina learned to teach patrons how to find needed materials rather than doing their research for them. Trying to provide effective library instruction was an ongoing challenge as colleagues presented very different examples of how much information and interaction to pack into the allotted time period. Becoming the library's liaison to the college of sciences and mathematics was intimidating to someone with a bumpy relationship to those areas during her own academic years. It took Tina a long time to stop apologizing to her classes for not understanding their topics; she finally recognized that explaining the use of library resources could be untangled from explaining the actual material held in those resources.

Some adjustments were due to the small size. There were eight or nine librarians and a handful of staff; the smallest place she had worked since the multi-type cooperative, and unlike that place, the small academic wasn't connected to other libraries. When disagreements simmered between individuals, the hard feelings seemed omnipresent because people had to work together so frequently. But when strong teams formed, as happened in technical services, a great amount was accomplished because the two or three librarians involved could communicate, brainstorm, make decisions, and solve problems quickly and creatively. Small size has the advantage of agility.

Still other changes were due to the university being private. Tina had only worked in public institutions before. Procurement processes differed. Without a governmental body to be a component of, and not closely affiliated to other schools, the university seemed like a world unto itself.

She encountered some prejudice toward her past in public libraries. There seemed to be a sense among a few colleagues that the work in public libraries was simpler and clerical rather than professional in nature. Tina found this baffling, given that she had been hired for the very experience that she had gained primarily in public libraries.

Discord amongst various camps within the library repeatedly waxed and waned over the years and it worsened toward the end of Tina's tenure there. She felt that colleagues were treated poorly because they weren't in the "in" camp. She sensed that she had done all she could with that job and only wanted to leave the fraught environment. A new job search began.

At this point, she had experienced a few libraries that were marred by various levels of toxicity. She would be hyper-attuned to atmosphere, interpersonal comments, and actions during her search. On the flip side, she was agnostic as to type or size of library, having had good experiences across the spectrum. She was also able to move, which broadened the available pool of jobs. The libraries to which she applied were publics, academics, and one multi-type, across the United States, and with sizes ranging very small to very large.

After numerous phone and video interviews, and in-person interviews at two public libraries and two universities, Tina was pleased to accept a job at a very large university. The appeal was an interesting, varied position with enough new elements to present a learning curve and a change from the past. The friendly, welcoming atmosphere was apparent throughout the daylong interview. Tina's experience fit what they were looking for and a good match was made.

Why switch?

We've looked at the path of one career. Let's now consider a more universal list of reasons that a change in library environment might make sense for you. Some of these would serve as motivation for any job change, including to an environment much like the one you're most familiar with. But your pool of potential positions will be so much greater if you're willing to broaden the initial set of requirements. Like helping a patron broaden a search, think of this as removing a confining term or two.

- There may be greater opportunities to advance your career. Maybe you're ready to move into a management role, but your current department head or director is unlikely move on. Perhaps you're a solo librarian or part of a very small staff. In such situations, moving to a larger library is the only way to work your way up the ranks.
- You may have to change libraries in order to use specialized skills or work with specific populations. One of our interviewees mentioned the desire to work with serious medical researchers. Another interviewee expressed his desire for a job where he could use his language skills.
- Another library environment may be the opportunity to change career focus. This may be the case if you're feeling like you've done all you can do in your current role, are intrigued by another part of the field, or want to go deep in something that's a small part of your current assignment. A different size can offer that change too. A smaller environment could let the full-time cataloger expand their skills to include all kinds of tech services work. A larger environment could give the public services librarian a chance to specialize in teen librarianship.
- Perhaps you have geographic constraints. The job market is generally most advantageous to those who have the flexibility to move. But if moving to another area is out of the question, then you must look at the libraries within commuting distance or opportunities to work online, such as "ask-a-librarian" chat services, contract cataloging, and institutions that permit employees to work remotely.
- Conversely, if you need to follow a spouse or partner's job, then you may need a job wherever you land, and must adjust your sights to the local market.
- A different library environment may be your best opportunity for accommodating personal needs such as part-time hours, summers off, or a flexible schedule.
- Perhaps you need to get away from your current library. If you're dealing with a toxic environment or sensing pending lay-offs, then the need to find another job may supersede any inclination toward a specific environment.

- Maybe you're bored. Feeling "been-there-done-that" all the time at work these days? Getting back on the learning curve in a new environment could solve that problem.
- Finally, you learn what you want from your job as you gain experience. Maybe you took a department head position but realize that you don't really like managing people (Hall, 2003). Perhaps you became a user-experience university librarian but realize now that the user experiences that most interest you are those of small children. If you feel your role is too narrow at a very large institution, maybe a small library where you wear many hats is a better fit. One of our interviewees, Shelly, mentioned this type of self-discovery: "there are a couple [library] directors in my area [who], from what I understand, they actually started out in what you would consider a more prestigious job and they made the choice to go to simpler, more solitary jobs in rural areas. And I find that interesting that what you think you want when you're out of library school and what you actually end up happy with are not necessarily the same things." Another interviewee, Kady, echoed this sentiment: "Well, you learn a lot about what you like and don't like by working at a lot of different libraries." She found a job she loves after several jobs and internships with aspects that she didn't love. A new environment could suit your newly clarified preferences, too.

Following up on this last bullet point, let's look at some factors that differ between library environments. Thinking about which elements speak to you is one step to determining the right path.

Differences (and similarities) in types and sizes of libraries

Satisfying professional experiences are available in a wide range of libraries, but there are differences that the librarian seeking a change should consider. While this is not an exhaustive list, we hope it will provide food for thought.

Philosophies about library activities

- Weeding and collection development policy: Many public libraries prioritize having popular and current titles. They weed heavily, getting rid of materials that are no longer in demand. However, many research libraries and special collections rarely or never weed. In some disciplines, the historical content remains highly relevant.
- Outreach to various groups within the community: The concept is the same, but the population groups differ. Public libraries may reach out to specific segments of their community, such as senior citizens, local businesses, homeschoolers, or makers, by planning events and programs. Academic libraries may reach out to their students with special events, as well as having a focused effort to connect with faculty.

- Reference: In public libraries, patrons come to the desk with questions that they need to find the answer to, and librarians are focused on helping them find that piece of information or a referral to an agency that can help. At academic libraries, the focus is instead on teaching information literacy skills and how to perform sound research.
- Collection development: In academic libraries, faculty will impact your purchasing choices at a rate beyond their percentage of the population because their reading lists and research heavily shape the needs of their students. In public libraries, various elements within the community are more evenly weighted (Hall, 2003). In special libraries, such as corporations, law firms, or specialized research institutes, you may be wholly focused on the needs of your primary researchers with no broader constituency. The size of your library in the sense of available shelf space, as well as options for remote storage and interlibrary lending/document delivery will impact collection decisions as well.
- Cataloging: the guidelines are the common factor. The types of materials obviously varies. The vendors also vary and that can impact issues like source of MARC records. Whether the librarian is cataloging one item at a time or working with large batches of records that require manipulation with various programs is another variable. Working within a library versus at a consortia hub or for a vendor that serves many libraries will impact your work life, how your work is prioritized, and potentially the speed at which you are expected to produce results.

Patron focus

- What factors distinguish your primary clientele?
  - Age
  - Place of residence
  - Course of study, teaching, or research
  - Place of business
  - Membership in the organization
  - Expert practitioner
  - Client
- What activities are they pursuing?
  - Leisure reading or watching
  - Complete an assignment
  - Write a dissertation
  - Find instructional materials for their students
  - Genealogy
  - Working and need data, studies, or information to support and further that work
  - Learning or building skills
  - Using the library as a remote work location

10 *A new size or type of library*

- Using the library to escape the elements or challenging home life
- Take a class, attend events or book groups, socialize
- What kind of materials, activities, classes and special services does the library provide them? See additional bullet points in this section.

Consortia or independent/single site or system

- As part of a consortia or system, you automatically have an additional layer(s) of colleagues to draw upon.
- The consortia may manage the ILS and other software tools, potentially relieving the library of those responsibilities but also potentially removing local control and choice.
- Purchasing may be controlled or managed at a central site, again relieving the local library of that task but also removing some level of local autonomy. Likewise, group licensing projects may be driven by a central site, offering potentially better deals but requiring that the library make selections in accordance with the group's choices.

Types of classes and events offered

- Teaching people to research in their area of specialization
- Teaching job searching skills
- Teaching technology skills at a variety of levels
- Teaching citation methods and how to avoid plagiarizing
- Arts and crafts for kids, teens, and adults; makerspaces both high-tech (3-D printers) and high-touch (learn to knit); life skills like cooking or budgeting
- Author/researcher/local expert talks
- Classes for new immigrants.

Services provided

- Provide tax forms, social workers, local government services, post office, package delivery, or test proctoring services
- Provide quiet study spaces
- Loan tools, games, puzzles, puppets, passes to local attractions
- Provide research appointments with a subject specialist
- Have publicly available computers, copiers, printers, fax, scanners, etc.
- Deliver documents or other materials to researcher or client
- Quick turnaround time on fact checking.

Collections: just a few models

- Popular, current materials
- Complete runs of popular and classic series and authors

- Support the currently taught curriculum
- Complete, comprehensive research collection with a small popular reading collection
- Perpetual access to electronic resources versus access only during the subscription period
- One copy of a bestseller or 300?
- Rare or unique materials
- Books by local authors – or by faculty authors
- Locally created music or video
- Textbooks

Size of library

- In a large library, you may specialize in one area of the profession and have specialist colleagues to consult with if your work overlaps. In a small institution, you are more likely to be a generalist who acquires pockets of specialized knowledge as needed. Do you prefer going deep and specializing, or being a "jack-of-all-trades"?
- Do you like to have sole authority and responsibility over a process/domain, or would you prefer to be one of a group? At the small university, Tina enjoyed being able to work the whole process of monographic technical services from acquisitions to writing MARC load tables to display in the discovery layer; she liked being able to improve the process until it was very efficient and met all the necessary goals. At the large university, those technical services responsibilities are spread out across multiple people in the university library and at the consortia headquarters which manages the ILS. Each librarian has control over a much smaller sphere of the process as a whole and has numerous colleagues with whom to collaborate.
- On the flip side, at the small university, Tina was encouraged to do reference, instruction, collection development, and faculty liaison work in addition to her technical services role. She learned a great deal about the breadth of university library activities and how they fit together; however, this range of responsibilities also left her with limited time for her primary areas of responsibility.
- A very small library may require coordination of vacation and professional leave time, due to the need to cover service points. At a large library, multiple people from one department may attend the same conference and still leave sufficient coverage in-house.
- Are you expected to be able to cover in other departments during busy times or when others are out? Is nearly everyone at nearly every meeting or are lots of things going on at your library that you're not even aware of?
- While many of the interviewees that the authors spoke to had moved from small to large libraries, Betsy Appleton discussed moving from large to small (Appleton & Buck, 2016; Appleton, Buck, and Seiler, 2017):

12   *A new size or type of library*

- Less hierarchy to work through. Things can be done more quickly, rather than needing to be discussed at multiple levels of administration.
- Quicker and easier to adjust procedure and processes because fewer people are involved.
- More involvement and awareness in other areas of librarianship. Topics that would have been the realm of a wholly separate department in the large library necessitated the input of all the librarians in the small one.
- Opportunity to get hands-on experience with systems that she didn't have rights to edit at the large library such as the ILS and discovery layer.
- Broader authority, broader responsibilities; she became more of a tech services generalist versus an electronic resources specialist.

• Sara reflected on changing library size: "I moved from a small community college library of five librarians to a very large university library with about 40 librarians. I've loved both library environments, and there are definite benefits to each. At the small library, we were very agile. We had a great team atmosphere, and worked together well, so when we wanted to make changes it was easy to communicate them to everyone and get everyone on board. Most issues we were addressing were library issues, so we only had to get library staff in the room to discuss what we wanted to do. At a large library, you're faced with a lot more bureaucracy. You can't always get everyone in the room to discuss what needs to be done, so instead you form committees who will look at possibilities and submit a report to the greater body. Then, perhaps you'll hold a vote, or maybe the committee itself will be the body that makes the decision. I've also been surprised at how much control I have over my actual job duties at a large library. Because we have so many more librarians and staff here, there are other people available to take on certain tasks. Additionally, because we are so large, there is always work that needs to be done, so if I wanted to take on duties that are outside of my department, it would be very easy for me to do this. At a small library, all of us did a little bit of everything. I didn't really enjoy working at the reference desk, but we all had to take shifts. It would not have been possible for me to say, 'I don't like working the desk, I'm not going to do it anymore.'"

Structure of parent organization and reporting structure outside the library

- In a university, the library may be part of a non-academic unit, such as information technology, reporting up through a vice-president of technology. Or, the library may be part of the academic side of the house, where the library dean reports to the provost.
- In a city or county library system, the library may be its own department, or it may be contained within a "leisure services" department along with

parks and recreation. In some municipalities, the public library is external to the city or town government, reporting to the elected library board.
- School librarians may work in multiple schools within a district that is independent or part of a city or county.

Working for vendors

Our interviewee, Deb, noted that she needed a different mindset when moving to the corporate environment to work for a library vendor. Among the changes: a faster pace; the need to make money for the corporation; and working for multiple libraries rather than only one. It also changed her career-long understanding of technical services standards: "There's a lot of contextual stuff that you have to consider when you're applying standards for your library, and I never ever realized that until I was working with so many libraries at once."

Rank

Academic librarian ranks can be confusing to the non-academic as well as to the new academic librarian. Often, the entry-level librarian starts as an instructor. A formal promotion process requires proof that the librarian has the necessary achievements in professional activities, scholarship, service (which we discuss in further detail in Chapter 3). The next level is usually Assistant Librarian. (The word "assistant" doesn't imply that the librarian is another person's assistant in the sense of an administrative assistant. It's simply the name of that level.) The next level of the ladder is Associate Librarian. The top rank is variously referred to as University Librarian (which sometimes refers to the library dean or director rather than a rank), Professor Librarian, or simply Librarian.

In public and government libraries, it is usually a simpler numbering system where rank is at least in part dependent on the length of service. A promotion in that context is typically a move to a different job, say a move up to management, whereas in the academic sense, the promotion in rank means that the librarian has the same job but is functioning at a higher level and their scholarship and service have greater scope and impact. At academics where librarians have a staff status, rank is likely more similar to the model in publics and government libraries.

Other options you may not have considered before

In addition to the variations discussed above, librarians have options beyond size and type that many people may not have considered before. Our interviewees and colleagues talked about multi-type library systems; temporary positions; the unique qualities of rural libraries; and libraries in developing countries.

Multi-types

Shelly is the director of a multi-type library organization that provides services to the libraries and librarians in her region of the United States. This kind of work may be appealing to those who are interested in dealing with many types of libraries. She says, "we work with all types of libraries, so I'm in contact with school librarians and public librarians and academic librarians. We do have a few special librarians in this area … They're mostly in museums." As mentioned in the beginning of this chapter, Tina worked in a similar agency and can vouch for the fun of interacting with many types of librarians and learning about their needs and interests.

Temporary or contract positions

Two of our interviewees, Ronit and Stewart, chose to take on temporary or contract positions to see what they liked. Ronit said,

> I think at first we're kind of ambivalent to take on contract positions; we obviously want a permanent position right away. But I kind of really enjoyed the fact that I got a couple different contract positions because it gave me the opportunity to try different positions and different libraries and get a feel for what works for me and what doesn't.

Stewart chose the same route after getting his MLS. "And then I made a deliberate decision to work in as many different kinds of libraries, types of libraries, as I could early on so I could decide which one I wanted." He has worked as a librarian in corporate, public, and academic libraries, as well as gaining experience in several specialties. "My career path is for people who don't know what to do," he says. "And so, working in different kinds of libraries was a really good experience for me." On the other hand, Meredith Schwartz argues in her editorial in the March 3, 2020 issue of *Library Journal* that "gig librarianship" has become a harmful trend, trapping some librarians in underpaid positions without health insurance (if in the United States) and needing numerous gigs to try to make ends meet. The full editorial is worth reading if this is a route that you're considering (Schwartz, 2020).

Rural libraries

Shelly spoke about the opportunities of working in a rural area in the American Upper Midwest:

> To get someone with a library degree into the area is difficult, and so they hire managerial types from within the community and those people just

stay. It's their community; they've often lived there all their lives. They have families, they have spouses, they don't have a reason to leave the area so they really don't want to even look at a larger library because that might be 20 miles away and in the winter it's hard to get there. People who have the library degrees, yes, especially if they want to work in public libraries or academic libraries, they come to this part of the country, they get a job that will give them their first experiences. They don't have to have a number of years' experience already in libraries.

Diane talked about working in a small town in a remote part of the American West. Sometimes teachers come from Chicago or Minneapolis.

And sometimes they really have a hard time dealing with the isolation, and the fact that ... we have to go 80 miles to a movie theater. Or that there's one grocery store, so that there's not a lot. And sometimes that's hard for people to deal with, that there's not a lot of choices ... Or the fact that if you want to go see your parents ... when [my parents] got sick, I couldn't be there in 2 hours; it was a 10-hour drive.

On the plus side, though, she said it's a great area for people who enjoy hunting, fishing, hiking, and other outdoor activities. Diane also extolled the value of getting involved in the community to forge bonds and get past any sense of isolation.

get involved with the community because it's small. Whether it's through your church, through civic organizations, or working with school activities and club. A long time ago, I was a cheerleading advisor and that was interesting because then you get to know people and do things. I did notice my first few years in [this town], sometimes I felt kind of isolated because people would talk about, oh, they got together with family and had dinner on Sunday and nobody ever invited me out to dinner. But I learned as I got involved and did stuff, joined a bowling team, did some other stuff, that I got to know people and then the invitations came and it felt more like home.

Maureen talked about the development of specialized library services to those in rural areas for populations with poor access to transportation.

So a pop-up library is where you go out and you have books on display and it might not be a location that people have transportation to get to a branch, so you're going to serve them where they are.

Her library brings books, programs, crafts, and other services to groups of seniors; families with children; and First Nation communities.

Libraries in developing countries

Pam worked in several countries beyond her native New Zealand, including two developing countries: Palau in Micronesia and Fiji. She recommends the experience.

> I'll just talk very briefly about [working] … in developing countries where things didn't work well, where the things that we take for granted as, you turn the light switch on and the light comes on. You can't guarantee that in a developing country. And there's potholes, and there's, the computer wasn't fantastic. There's sort of negatives sometimes moving into a different environment where you're bringing your skills in to an environment where people don't have that understanding, but you're having to accommodate a lot for the environment that you're in. So I felt it was very enriching to go into a developing country, and it was very meaningful because I basically had, the public library setting in particular, you can really change a person's life, actually in an academic library too, you get somebody who has nothing. I mean a lot of, in Fiji for example, in Fiji in particular, it's not a very poor Pacific country, but in a lot of households there were no books at all, or the only book they had was their religious text. So, libraries in that setting are very, very important, it's not just an additional "nice to have" kind of situation, that's actually what can change a person's life. And somebody who gets access to resources can even outside an academic context can learn how to grow their vegetables, their livelihood, do better in their own sort of personal life, and somebody who's studying for a qualification to actually bring their family out of poverty is really life changing. You make more of a difference in a developing country, so it's actually worth some of the negatives that you get. And I'll just tell you a little anecdote, which is when I was in Palau, the librarian of the community college, she was actually an ex-pat librarian and she had to go back to the US. And so, they had to advertise the position. And I put it onto some of the IFLA (International Federation of Library Associations and Institutions) job advertisement lists, and I got approached by several people in the US who were interested in the position. But one of them just said that he was sure that I must have typed the salary wrong because it couldn't possibly be, and this was in about 2007, it couldn't possibly be 22,000 US dollars, could it. And I had to reply and say yes that is the salary. And the only thing I could say to him was that it includes free accommodation. Never heard from him again. And he obviously just, and obviously it was a terrible salary, and it was the same salary I was on. We didn't do it for the money … I was able to go snorkeling every weekend, and some of the best snorkeling and diving sites in the world. There were just some amazing benefits which you didn't necessarily think about. We just had some really amazing experiences

which I never would have had if I had just stayed in my own environment. So I do recommend, if people are – in fact a lot of the expat librarians I met were often older librarians, that obviously been in roles where they sort of saved, they had a reasonable retirement planned, but they wanted to give themselves an interesting last few years before they retired, and that's actually a really excellent opportunity to get out there and to just explore the world, and to share the decades of experiences you've got with the countries where they don't have that sort of depth of knowledge. So. I really recommend people to think about that sort of thing in their last few years before they retire.

She also had a colleague who chose to start his career working in a library in a developing country:

one of his first roles was actually in Fiji as a librarian there, and he came from the UK and met his wife in Fiji and then moved on to live in New Zealand. And he started his career like that, and other people have finished their career like that, and I do think it's a great opportunity. It really makes a difference to how you view the world, because you're not just a tourist there, you're actually working alongside people with quite different cultural environments, and it's such an amazing opportunity to really step outside your comfort zone and learn the most amazing things as a result.

Misconceptions about other library environments

Some librarians have encountered the misconception that librarians have to remain in the same segment of the industry for their entire career. Thankfully, not everyone has subscribed to this concept and its prevalence has diminished over time. Some misconceptions persist and may hinder people in their career considerations. The librarian who is interested in changing environments might want to be aware of these misconceptions and be assured that others see them as being inaccurate.

One such misconception is that work in small libraries lacks the complexity and/or sophistication of similar work in larger ones. In a similar vein, academic librarians sometimes think that public library work is simpler. Complexities exist in each situation. The differences may simply be not obvious to the uninitiated. For example, a large academic may have six or eight individuals involved in a demand-driven video program. A variety of individuals select content, track licenses, pay invoices, catalog and optimize the catalog/discovery layer, assess statistics, and make renewal and de-selection decisions. Much of the complexity there lies in accurate and timely communication between the many parties. A small library may have two people doing that full sequence of work. The complexity here is gaining enough mastery of numerous skills.

Another example of a misconception is that academic librarians are sheltered from difficult patron interactions. While public librarians likely interact with a higher percentage of people who represent a wide range of potential challenges, academics are faced with the mental health challenges becoming increasingly prevalent on college campuses today. Also, many academic libraries are open to the public, particularly at community colleges and publicly funded institutions. In short, challenging patron interactions happen in all libraries, and all face the need for training and support to improve safety and enhance community well-being (Resources for Public Libraries Serving Persons Experiencing Homelessness, 2018).

One of our interviewees, Kathy, encountered misconceptions about library school graduates who had attended programs that had a reputation for strong public library tracks. Some thought those candidates wouldn't fare as well in academia. But Kathy has found this to be baseless.

Tina found herself in a discussion with other academic serials librarians about potential collaborations with public librarians who work with serials. Many of the other academics voiced assumptions that serials work in public libraries is very simple, such as shelving new issues of popular magazines or subscribing to a popular-magazine database. Tina spoke up about her experience that the complexities are different in the different environments. In the academic world, her serials work concerns include binding, perpetual access, linking, Open Access, knowledge base, and "big deals," whereas in the public library, it included collection management of thousands of print subscriptions for nearly 30 locations; adjusting collection size and scope based on branch size and community demographics; delivery problems; and gift subscriptions from local patrons. Another academic librarian spoke of the work done by one of her parents, who was a public librarian. It wasn't simple. Were any opinions changed during this conversation? Unknown. But the seeds were planted. The conversations need to continue.

Librarian impressions of changing types: survey results

The authors found very little in the professional librarian literature about librarians changing size or type of library. To learn more about other librarians' perceptions and experiences of moving to another type of library, we conducted a survey in the summer of 2019. Invitations to participate were sent to numerous library email lists and more than 1,700 librarians filled out the survey. A summary of the results follows, and the full survey and results are in Appendix A.

Perception of bias against hiring librarians from another type of library

Most librarians surveyed think there is some bias against hiring librarians from another type of library. This perception is nearly identical between librarians who have worked in one type of library (57% say there is a bias) and those who have worked in two or more types (59% perceive a bias.) The differences are more substantial if we break out the "one-library-type" librarians. Those who work in four-year academics are most likely to say there is a bias, with 70% saying yes, while government librarians are least likely to perceive a bias, with 45% saying yes.

Perception of whether library skills transfer easily between types

A majority of librarians think that library skills transfer easily between types. In total, 53% of one-type librarians agree with this, while 58% of the two-or-more-type librarians agreed. Only 4% and 3%, respectively, said that skills don't transfer easily; all the rest said, "it depends." What does it depend on? Many people stated that it depends on the individual. Here is a sampling of other free-text responses given.

- "Skills can transfer easily, but whether or not they do depends on the librarian in question. Even transferring to a new department within a library type you have to be willing to understand and adjust to your new context. Sometimes people do this naturally and the skills then transfer and develop into the new role naturally. Other times people do not recognise the need to learn and understand the new environment fully, and this can make it difficult for them to adapt and grow into the new role."
- "Customer service focus and core ethics translate very well, in my experience. There can be a learning curve in other areas (like systems, collection development, etc.)"
- "on the type of position for example a reference librarian at public library can more easily transition to an instruction position at an academic library than a cataloger from the same type of library."
- "I think that cataloging skills, for example, would translate easily. Reference skills, on the other hand, wouldn't as easily because the nature of reference questions differs widely between, say, academic libraries and public libraries."
- "There is bias, and the skill sets do vary widely. That said, there's an awful lot less bias today than when I started in this career, and a greater recognition of the skills and strengths professionals from other sectors bring in."
- "On how deeply the librarian is holding on to the rules and regulations of their former library."
- "Public, academic and corporate institutions all have quirks. The base skills may transfer but the work environments are very different."
- "I think it's more about the size of the library than the type of library."
- "In my experience, the skills are job specific and not library type specific"
- "We do not hire on library specific skills or qualifications, rather communication, research, leadership and relationship-building skills."

- "Skills do but behaviours and attitudes are harder to shape – e.g. HE [higher education] very much about helping users help themselves, government is about doing everything for the customer."
- "The attitude of the librarian in question is the primary variable. They must be open to learning new skills and adapting skills they have."
- "I don't think it's easy necessarily. They are different environments with different resources, cultures, and thus skills and mindset needs to adapt and change when you transition. It can cause a person to question their skills and 'fitness' for the library world in general."
- "Skills transfer but specialist knowledge needs to be acquired. e.g. I am dealing with very different resources at a high school library than I did at an academic library. Especially knowledge of YA literature! So always some upskilling."
- "If the hiring library is not condescending towards the candidate the move can occur smoothly."
- "There are some idiosyncrasies by type (especially philosophy and process), but most of the basic skills transfer."

Perception of whether librarians should be open to moving across library types in the course of their career

Librarians who have worked in one type of library generally think that librarians should be open to changing types. Only 1% said that changing types is a bad idea or that success is rare. In total, 35% said "maybe," 14% said "yes, but be careful," and 50% think it's often a good idea.

Librarians who have worked in more than one type of library are even more strongly positive. A total of 0% think it's a bad idea or that success is rare, 26% said "maybe" librarians should consider moving across types, 13% said "yes, but be careful," while a whopping 61% think it's often a good idea.

Has your current library hired librarians from a different environment in the past five years?

Librarians who have worked in one type of library were less likely to have colleagues hired from other environments in the previous five years. In total, 46% said their library had made such a hire, 40% said their library had not, and 14% weren't sure.

Conversely, 59% of librarians who have worked in more than one type said that their libraries had hired from other types in the previous five years. A total of 23% were in libraries that had not made such a hire and 18% were unsure.

Interviewees' takes on changing environments

In addition to the survey results, we also want to share a number of quotes from our interviewees. Let their advice and insights encourage and support you as you move along this process.

Kat moved around the United States several times due to her husband's work and she worked in a variety of environments over the course of those moves. She said: "What I would recommend is be open to whatever opportunities might happen ... whatever happens with family, with your spouse, you have to be flexible and just be ready for whatever opportunity might be there."

Yolanda said:

> don't feel like your career path has to follow anything. Do what feels good to you, do what you're going to be interested in, do what you like. So many people have said to me, why would you leave – I was at [a university in the United States] and I was tenured and promoted – and so people were like, why would you leave a tenure track position to go to [a different university] which doesn't have tenure? And I was like, because the position sounded great, it's [a desirable location], the people were really nice when I interviewed. So, I always tell people – or try to tell people – that you have to do what you think you're going to love and what you think you're going to be passionate about. So I don't think you should have in mind that, oh, I'm going to follow this trajectory of doing this and then this and then this. Like I'm going to do librarianship and then I'm going to go into middle management and then I'm going to be an administrator. Like, you can follow that and there's nothing wrong with that, but don't be afraid to choose something that feels completely different and off-track because that's how you get to do the stuff that's fun and that you love and makes it feel like it's not a job at all.

Stewart said:

> difficulties (in transitioning between libraries) are mostly perceptual on the part of the employers ... [T]he difficulties in transition have more to do with the corporate culture of a given place than with either the subject matter or the practices. It's work, but you can do it. You find the tools and learn to use them. Take a course or online training or webinar ... The more challenging part is figuring out the sort of social engineering of just how things are done here.

Maureen supported the idea that you grow over time, and that your capabilities and interests change, too. Maureen started off as a cataloger fresh out of library school. She was shy at this point in her life and being in the back-office suited her. As she gained experience and confidence, that changed.

> I was starting to come out of my shell. But when I was cataloging, I also started teaching Aquacise and aerobics, and that gradually brought me out and made me more comfortable in terms of speaking in front of larger groups, etc., and then I just grew from there. So, all my steps after the cataloging years have just added on, added on, added on.

She added that branching out in her professional role, now as a library director of a rural library, contributes to her still being excited to come to work and if she had remained in cataloging for her entire career, she would likely have burnt out. She recommends: "be diverse in what you do, like don't just pigeonhole yourself in."

Sonia emphasized a willingness to learn. Recounting her transition from simultaneous part-time positions as a public children's librarian and academic social sciences librarian to a law librarian, she says anyone can do it:

> I think anyone can [make a transition between library types] if they are kind of open and willing to learn, because I know it was a big steep learning curve for me. But I mean I was willing to do it, and I was actually, on my own time, I was reading about the law. For about a year and a half, all my reading was really about law. So, if you are willing to do it, I think everyone is capable; it depends on how much effort you are willing to put on that.

Pam, a library science instructor, recognizes the value in some people remaining in one library or one type for their whole career, "because they're just building up a lot of very specific knowledge that is great for the institution." However, she says:

> there are huge benefits in actually moving to different types of institutions and learning more about how libraries operate in a different setting, and possibly even sharing it backwards. One of the things which I have really enjoyed is I keep contact with my people in different institutions I've worked in ... We do all this networking all the time; you ask them questions and you share information about things you've both learned and such like. There's a lovely kind of symmetry, I suppose, in finding out what you think is so different actually isn't.

Stewart further advised:

> reexamine what is making you want to leave one type of library and go to another. Is it a push or is it a pull? If it's a push, think really carefully about what it is that's pushing you out because it could be at the place you go just as easily. If it's a pull, that's different. If it's something that's attracting you to another kind of library work, then that's actually a better reason to switch from one library type to another.

He gave several examples of potential "pulls": for more money, consider a corporate library; for prestige, consider an Ivy League school; if you want to work with serious researchers, look for schools or institutes with such a reputation.

Deb advises:

> Don't be afraid of it. There are opportunities; there are more similarities than there are differences between the different fields of librarianship, for lack of a better term, different silos. And I think that there's a lot to be gained by bringing your experience from one area to another.

What is to come in the rest of this book

In Chapter 2, we'll expand our topic to look at further concepts and options for career re-invention. Chapter 3 moves to the realities of a job search and provides lots of practical guidance and advice about résumés, CVs (curriculum vitae), and interviewing, plus support for when it doesn't work out or takes longer than you expect. Chapter 4 explores another means of support: mentorship. We encountered many different concepts of mentorship as we talked with people about our topic and we're eager to share these ideas for relationships that help both of you grow and improve. Chapter 5 talks about being The New Person. You've got that new job and now you're the newbie. It's exciting but stressful and we have some tips to help cope. Chapter 6 furthers the discussion of handling stresses and emotions on the job. Chapter 7 sees you settling in and ready to look at expanding your professional reach with publishing, presenting, and service. Finally, in Chapter 8, we sum things up, look at the current and (potentially) future state of libraries, and send you off with some more wisdom from our interviewees.

References

Appleton, B., & Buck, T. H. (2016, April). Size Does(n't) Matter: Growing Your Career in a Wildly Different Organization. Presentation at the Electronic Resources & Libraries (ER&L) Conference, Austin, Texas.

Appleton, B., Buck, T.H. & Seiler, C. (2017). Change It Up: Growing Your Career in a Wildly Different Organization. *Roll with the Times, or the Times Roll Over You: 2016 Proceedings of the Charleston Library Conference* (pp. 378–383) Purdue University Press. https://doi.org/10.5703/1288284316475

Duff, S. & Buck, T.H. (2019). Survey on Librarian Career Path and Attitudes. Conducted via Qualtrics software provided by University of Central Florida.

Hall, M. L. (2003). Public to Academic: Reflections for Librarians Who Are Considering the Switch. *Public Libraries*, 42(3), 154–156.

Resources for Public Libraries Serving Persons Experiencing Homelessness. (2018 February). American Library Association, www.ala.org/pla/resources/tools/homelessness

Schwartz, M. (2020, March 3). Gig Librarianship. *Library Journal.* www.libraryjournal.com/?detailStory=Gig-Librarianship-Editorial

Further reading

Franks, T. P. (2017). Should I Stay or Should I Go? A Survey of Career Path Movement within Academic, Public and Special Librarianship. *Journal of Library Administration*, 57(3), 282–310. https://doi.org/10.1080/01930826.2016.1259200

Franks, T. P. (2019). Career Path Movement: Perspectives about Transitioning Between Library Environments. *Journal of Library Administration*, 59(5), 475–491. https://doi.org/10.1080/01930826.2019.1616974

Franks, T. P., Budzise-Weaver, T. & Reynolds, L. J. (2017). Unlocking Library Search Committees at ARL Public Universities: Techniques and Best Practices for Getting Hired. *Information and Learning Science*, 118(5/6), 252–265. https://doi.org/10.1108/ILS-04-2017-0024

Gold, H. (2016). At Least You Didn't Burn the Place Down: Leadership Isn't for Everyone. *College & Research Libraries News*, 77(10), 502–503. https://doi.org/10.5860/crln.77.10.9571

Saunders, L. & Jordan, M. (2013). Significantly Different? Reference Services Competencies in Public and Academic Libraries. *Reference and User Services Quarterly*, 52(3), 216.

2 Exploring new opportunities

Every librarian can take measures to reinvent or reinvigorate their career, even if they are not ready to leave their current job. From scouring job ads to cross-training with other departments, there are many ways to find and acquire new skills. Many tutorials for in-demand skills can be found freely online with a little bit of digging. Librarians should make a plan for themselves by compiling a list of skills or experience they need, and then determine where they can gain that knowledge. By making such a plan, the librarian will be prepared for the next job or promotion down the line. This chapter suggests ways to explore the profession such as reading about trends, looking at job postings, and keeping up with the professional literature. At work, the librarian can explore cross-training, study the library's new initiatives, and take steps to customize their job.

In this chapter we'll talk about reinventing your career. You may be ready to start that reinvention at a new library or you might be looking for options from a position you've held for a while. You can begin your reinvention by exploring opportunities at your existing institution, volunteering with professional organizations, attending conferences, and networking.

Exploring the profession

Trends

Reading about new library trends and innovations can help stimulate the imagination. One way to start is to look at awards given to librarians with innovative ideas and projects. You're unlikely to be inspired by every single one of these libraries and librarians but looking through the lists can spark new ideas and help you hone your library philosophy. Some awards post essays by the winning librarians or short explanations of how they've been innovative. In other cases, a little web searching is needed to get more information about the project. Consider if any of the ideas might be suitable for your current library or if they start to point you in the direction you want to go. Here are some helpful places to look:

- Charleston Library Conference "Fast Pitch" https://charlestonlibraryconference.com/fastpitch/ Scroll to the lower part of the page for information about past winners and runners-up.
- Awards granted to Public Library Association libraries and librarians: www.ala.org/pla/awards
- UK Serials Group Innovation Awards: www.uksg.org/news/15-10-2019/InnovationAwards
- Library Journal's "Movers and Shakers" www.libraryjournal.com/?subpage=movers

Look at job postings

Whether you're already nestled in your new job or simply looking for options, scanning job descriptions is a great way to spot trends in your area and gaps in your own skillset. Look for ads from institutions that you consider to be innovators and/or position titles that seem to have been updated with the times. You'll particularly want to look at the required and preferred skills and experience. Does anything tug at you? What comes up again and again but is unfamiliar to you? Write these things down in a list of things to pursue.

Let's break the items on your lists into two categories. First, take a look at things you can actively pursue now, such as getting training or getting experience in the shorter term. For example, you may be able to get training on a piece of software – or at least that category of software, even if neither the product nor the training is available from your institution. There may be options from a product's homepage, such as a monthly subscription to training materials; maybe a short-term outlay is worth it to you. Freely available options include YouTube and technology-centered websites, both for the specific product and the category. Of course, you may also find books and magazine articles about software products. This sort of ad-hoc self-training is most accessible for product categories that are widely used beyond the library industry, such as data visualization or image editing software, but you should be able to find some form of training on just about every software on the market. For each skill you want to seriously pursue, make a curriculum of these various webinars, tutorials, or books, and even a timeline to view or read each if you want a detailed plan.

A type of experience you could feasibly get is supervisory experience. You may not be able to get a full-time employee assigned to report to you, but perhaps you could get a student worker, volunteer, or intern. Develop a plan for what this person would actually do, both day-to-day and big picture, and a tentative timeframe for how long the work would last, then approach your supervisor. If this isn't possible, consider ways that you could supervise part of someone's work, such as overseeing one specific task or project within your area of expertise. Even temporary supervisory experience can be helpful, such as managing a student assistant or volunteer when their regular supervisor is out of the office for a few weeks.

The second category is things you can learn a little about, either to prepare yourself for future job interviews or in preparation for a longer-term project. There are fewer freely available training options for library-specific tools like a proprietary ILS versus non-library-specific software systems. Official training materials tend to be limited to staff in subscribing libraries, but we did find documentation for staff on a few library websites when we searched for the names of various products. It's also possible to learn about library products on non-product-specific email lists, discussion platforms like ALA Connect, and library journal articles. If you attend a library conference, ask for product demonstrations or even a sandbox account. Another kind of learning is talking with former colleagues or classmates who are engaged in the kind of work that interests you but that your library isn't currently engaged in. Sara talked to friends at other institutions when she wanted to learn about evidence-based acquisitions and hear specific examples of the benefits incurred by the libraries, as it wasn't something she could actually implement at the institution where she was then employed. This helped her understand some of the motivations of larger libraries, which was great preparation for interviewing with such a library.

Reading

It seems obvious to suggest to librarians that they explore new reading material when they're ready for something new, but sometimes we need to be reminded! Changing institution type or job focus (or both) will likely change your professional reading list. For instance, when Deb moved from a management role at a health sciences library to a business-development role at a library vendor, she told us that she increased the amount of business material she was reading. When moving from a monographs-focuses technical services role to one centered on serials and other continuing-resources, Tina subscribed to a serials-centered email list (SERIALST, currently hosted by NASIG: www.nasig.org/SERIALST) and to table-of-contents email notifications for *Serials Review* and *The Serials Librarian*. (Many publishers have this option to be notified of a new journal issue or of newly available articles, regardless of whether you or your library are subscribed.) Your library, or a neighboring public or academic library, may have a library and information-science focused database that can provide articles of interest as well as a way to explore the literature and find additional resources to feed your reinvention. Even if you can't get access to a full issue of a relevant journal you'd like to read, just reading through the table of contents and any free or open access articles can sometimes give you ideas of things to explore further.

At the library

Cross-training

Cross-training is a relatively low-stakes, hands-on way to help you decide if you're interested in moving to another part of the profession, expand your toolkit, or get a fresh perspective. Opportunities for cross-training may be available whether you're new to the library or not. If you're new, your job description and workload may be somewhat flexible at the beginning and able to move a bit with your interests. If you're well-established in your role, you may be efficient enough to be able to free up a few hours each week. Where you choose to pursue cross-training is a matter of personal preference and the situation in your library, such as whether the department needs help and/or if they have someone available to do the training and provide a project.

If cross-training isn't available, or if you want to explore further before committing to it, find time to chat with colleagues whose work intrigues you. Ask about the scope of their responsibilities, their projects, what's important to them, and what concerns them. Depending on your level of interest, you may want to ask what professional reading material, conferences, and professional associations they favor.

At the start of your job, you might have opportunities or even requests to participate in a work role outside your official one. For example, both authors had, and still have, the option of doing a few hours a week of reference and research assistance in addition to their regular jobs in the Acquisitions and Collection Services work. If you supervisor is okay with it, then this sort of option might be a good opportunity to explore another part of the profession, learn about another area of your library, and interact with colleagues you wouldn't see much otherwise. Taking advantage of opportunities versus making sure you don't get overextended is always a balancing act. Before accepting such an opportunity, find out how to reverse the decision if you begin to feel the additional role is detracting from your primary one.

New initiatives

What new projects is the library taking on? Getting involved in a new initiative or serving on the first iteration of a committee are all good fodder for someone seeking reinvention. Sometimes you can partake of these opportunities simply because you asked to be involved. Extra hands (and brains) are often welcome, whether you bring relevant knowledge, experience, or simply a willingness to figure stuff out. Not everyone wants to take on new challenges, so stepping up may be all it takes to be involved. For example, Tina was able to get herself on the system migration team when she worked as a cataloger at a public library. In part, this was due to her experience with migrations at previous jobs, and in part, it seemed, because her department head preferred not to be on the team.

Looking at planning documents can open your eyes to potential areas of reinvention. Some of this information might be in annual reports, minutes from administrative meetings, or other formally issued documents; it may require some investigation as to whether they exist and whether they're available to you. Alternatively, you may need to talk with your supervisor or ask other administrative figures as appropriate. The big questions: what are the up-and-coming areas or the fast-growing areas? What institutional or governmental requirements will lead to changes at the library and what opportunities might arise from this? An example from the university where the authors work is the area of textbook affordability. There was a state mandate about textbook affordability and the librarians were eager to make library-purchased eBooks more widely known to faculty and students as potential textbooks. Numerous librarians got involved in the various aspects of textbook affordability, including presenting at national conferences about it.

Making the job yours

There are numerous ways to make a job your own. Perhaps the most obvious is when you're the first incumbent in a newly created job. Frequently, positions are recast when a librarian leaves; the changes range from modest to substantial but typically seem to include a new title and different mix of responsibilities reflecting changes in the field and/or library. Other times a brand-new job is created based on newly identified library needs. In that case, you're the first to hold that job, with no predecessor to whom you can be compared. Within the scope of what's required, you choose which aspects to relish and enhance and which to minimize, and those choices will come to define the job. Along with that freedom comes the lack of precedent – you must figure things out from scratch because they've never been done before (at least in that library). In this scenario, you're either changing jobs within your existing library or you've moved to another library.

Another way to make a job your own is more incremental. You update your existing job over time, picking up new skills and responsibilities that both increase your know-how and improve library processes and offerings. Maybe new types of library materials have come to prominence and become an increasingly important part of your role; Sara has experienced this with acquisitions of streaming videos. Old duties of marginal benefit are left behind or die off. In this scenario, you're staying in the same "home" and renovating it as time passes. Make sure that your official job description and annual evaluation reflect these changes. This makes it easier to either move to another position or to make the case in-house for a promotion or raise.

A third type of change may sound a bit Machiavellian but is just looking out for your own interests. Sometimes a colleague leaves and aspects of their job would fit really well into your own, opening up a new avenue of potential exploration. Let's illustrate this with an example. Tina knew a librarian who was hired into a print serials librarian job. The duties included cataloging, acquisitions, and oversight of print serials shelf maintenance. This was in an era when print was a larger piece of the serials pie than it often is today, but the tide was already turning toward electronic journals. A year or two in, the electronic resources librarian announced her resignation. The serials librarian initiated a few conversations and ultimately the electronic resource management job was incorporated into the serials job (with a title change, of course.) Non-ERM aspects of the resignee's job were distributed among public services staff. Some routine aspects of the serials librarian job were identified and a lower level employee was trained. A new job was born. The incumbent was happy with the heightened opportunity to learn and grow, and administration was happy to have a vacant position that could be recast as needed.

This type of transformation doesn't always require someone to leave a job. In many libraries, librarians have aspects or tasks in their job that they would willingly jettison to another interested party. This is a delicate balance, however, as many people don't want to widely admit that they're unhappy with some part of their job, but in a close department where people feel secure in their jobs, this can be a normal part of yearly discussions.

There are surely other ways to make a job your own but hopefully these illustrations give you food for thought about opportunities you could take advantage of, whether you choose to stay or move on. The key aspects are to notice the ongoing changes within your part of the profession, keep your eyes open for the chance to update your skills and knowledge, and put those new abilities to work.

Professional development

Professional associations

Perhaps it's time to refresh your usual methods of professional development. Consider which conferences you attend. (Chapter 7 has a more in-depth discussion of conferencing if you're new to it.) Is it time to try different options? Make note of the library conferences you've heard of in passing and spend a little time investigating them online. Ask colleagues whose jobs intersect with yours what conferences they've attended, which ones they've found most helpful, and which they're intrigued by. Reach out to email lists, discussion platforms, and colleagues at other institutions, too. Partner with colleagues in different departments and submit a proposal to a conference in their area that you wouldn't normally attend.

Look into training opportunities offered by the library and by other departments in the broader institution such as human resources and information technology. There may be other opportunities specific to your area, such as project management software, handling challenging patrons, and working with the organization's financial system. Or, there may be more general training, such as how to be a good supervisor, ways to improve communication, or how to use basic office software more effectively.

Also look outside the immediate environment for training and growth opportunities (and chances to meet new colleagues). Is the library part of any consortia? Whether it's a group of libraries in the same geographical area, using the same ILS, or with another connection (such as a religious order or common research or patron base), see what opportunities are available. Be open to trying, even once, serving on a committee, taking a webinar or class, or attending an annual meeting.

Networking

Many of our interviewees mentioned opportunities that arose because of people they talked with during professional networking. Shelly told us that she got a call to interview for a job she hadn't even applied for because the library knew she was looking. Some got mentoring opportunities; others received insights about specific workplaces; and Kat got a job reviewing graphic novels because of the passion and expertise demonstrated though years of posting on a specialized email list. (See Chapter 7 for more on networking.)

Breaking this idea down into specifics, there are numerous kinds of networking:

- Go to conferences and workshops in person and do more than just attending sessions. Chat with fellow session attendees. Talk to presenters whose topic is relevant to your work or library. It's fine just to thank them for doing the presentation. It's also fine to ask a follow-up question or two; share a comment; or ask if you could follow up after the conference via email. Chat with fellow attendees at coffee breaks and meals. Ask questions during presentations. Share a thought during discussions. Some people won't be interested in chatting with you, and that's perfectly fine. Chat with someone else. There will be people at any librarian gathering who are either working on something related to your own work or who have an aspiration or problem similar to one you're dealing with or have perhaps solved. These interactions may last a friendly moment or two, or they could lead to longer-term professional connections.
- Participate on email discussion lists. If you have expertise, share it. If you have questions, ask.
- Volunteer to serve on committees. Whether a regional, national, or international library association; consortia; or your governing body, there are likely committees that need willing helpers. These may be in-person, online, or hybrid experiences. Approach tasks with friendly curiosity and fulfill your commitments as promised and you'll quickly become a valued team member who people will be pleased to encounter when the next opportunity arises.

32 *Exploring new opportunities*

Our interviewees have had numerous experiences with and advice about networking. Kady suggests trying to be around the people whose work you're interested in pursuing.

> If you're looking at a time of transition, if you can afford to, attend ALA, or if you want to get into public libraries, PLA. Or if you want to get into really specific collection work, if you can swing it, to go to Charleston. That would probably be the advice of just networking in those areas where people are already gathering ... I also found that librarians are very generous with their time. So, if you reached out to people and asked to just chat with them, I'm sure they would. But in a conference setting, you can be like, you're already here, and you're probably bored between sessions.

Fred has been involved in numerous professional associations throughout his career and those connections have been beneficial. He mentioned a multi-type association that served libraries of all types in the metropolitan area where he works.

> So, I had attended various meetings and actually organized something, I guess a seminar ... [and] on the panel was the person who was going to be my boss in the future. So that's how when the application came across the desk, she said, ah, I think I recognize the name. So that's always good.

Fred also got involved in different organizations to pursue relevant needs and interests. PLA benefitted his transition to and subsequent work in public libraries. The ACRL European Studies Section benefitted his involvement with languages. His state library association lets him serve as a mentor to new librarians. ALA has a committee where he can connect with others who also work with immigrants and refugees.

Jodie found great value in belonging to ALA, her state association, and the state's school librarian/library media specialist association.

> and so, all of those helped because it exposes you to the outside world and you know you're not alone. When you're the only person, the only children's librarian or the only [library] CEO or the only school librarian in the building, you sometimes feel like you're alone ... So, having the outside world connections are very, very important.

Questions for reflection

1. What other areas of librarianship would you like to learn more about?
2. What skills would you like to be able to add to your resume or CV?
3. For those on the technical side of the library, list at least three skills or software programs that you would like to learn.

Exploring new opportunities 33

4. For those in public services, list at least three new populations you're interested in reaching out to and/or programming ideas for those groups.
5. Are there any changes coming to your library that you know about?
6. Are you involved in networking within the library profession? Might other committees or organizations be worth exploring as part of your reinvention? While some have membership costs, others, such as IFLA, permit anyone to participate in their email lists.

3 Preparing for interviews and promotion

The job search is a stressful time, even when not applying to a different type or size of library. Preparing materials for submission to a job ad can be a source of anxiety and confusion. Librarians applying to a new type of library may not know what is expected of them as they work on their curriculum vitae (CV) or résumé. Additionally, interviews can vary widely depending on the type or size of library. It can be difficult for librarians to know what is standard if they are departing from their previous experience. Extra preparation at the outset can help librarians know what to expect and how they will be evaluated throughout the application and interview process. This chapter discusses each part of the résumé or CV and contains sample cover letters that show how to customize for each job. This chapter also gives advice for job interviews including contextualizing your past in a different environment. It gives tips for laying the groundwork for your future career moves, such as how to keep your application documents up to date. The chapter also shares tips from interviewees who have management and hiring experience. It concludes with questions for reflection.

Introduction

Tina applied for her faculty-rank university library job with a concise business-style résumé that was the norm in her previous institutions. Years later, she found that a curriculum vitae (CV) was necessary to apply for promotion in rank at the university. Only then did she learn what a CV actually entails and how much it differs from a résumé. Her three-page résumé quadrupled in length as the expected material and formatting was added. She realized that she should have applied for her current job with a CV but simply had no idea that the two terms represented such different documents.

This chapter is intended to help you avoid similar gaffes and misunderstandings with résumés and CVs as well as other aspects of job search and career mobility. With real-world examples and insights from our interviewees, we will see how a librarian can best represent their experience.

Whether you need a CV or a résumé, that document should be submitted with a cover letter. We will look at how to contextualize your experience in light of the job you're applying for. Pointing out parallels between your experiences and the qualifications in a job ad at another kind of library helps the search committee or hiring personnel better understand your abilities and accomplishments.

Moving along the job search process, we'll discuss interviewing. Then we look at laying the groundwork for a future job or promotion. We conclude with additional resources and items for reflection.

Letting go of perfection

It's easy to become obsessed with every detail of your résumé/CV, cover letter, and any other application materials that you are putting together. We offer a lot of details in this chapter that could contribute to becoming overwhelmed. Please don't feel that you need to worry over everything mentioned; we are accounting for numerous scenarios. Pick the items that feel most relevant to your situation and go forward with your application. As the saying goes, the perfect is the enemy of the good.

Résumé versus curriculum vitae (CV)

Curriculum vitae (CV) is Latin for "course of life." In contrast, résumé is French for summary (Internship and Career Center, University of California, Davis, 2018). These simple definitions get to the heart of the difference between the two documents. The CV details one's life work, typically starting from the oldest and moving forward in time. It covers the librarian's professional accomplishments, research and creative activities, and service work. Since it covers the course of a professional life, the CV can span many pages. In contrast, the résumé summarizes the librarian's professional experience, typically starting with the most recent and working backwards. Education and experience in the distant past are listed very concisely and some may be omitted if the applicant deems them irrelevant or too age-revealing. The résumé highlights the job candidate's knowledge, skills, and abilities in no more than three to four pages.

Public, school, and corporate library jobs typically require a résumé. Colleges and universities usually require a CV. At community colleges (that is, a two-year degree-granting institution), the required document often correlates to whether the librarians are faculty (CVs are probably the norm) or staff (either is likely acceptable.) It's best to be certain of the requirements before submitting your documents to a search process. If the application specifications aren't clear, consider inquiring if you have any doubt.

There are also cultural differences so plan to do extra research if applying to a library in a different country or region with another linguistic tradition. According to the University of California, Davis, Internship and Career Center, the term CV can be used to describe all job applications in Europe, while CV and résumé are sometimes used interchangeably in the United States and Canada (2018).

Arguably, submitting a résumé for an academic faculty position worked out just fine for Tina. She got the job and loves it. Consider, however, that her incoming rank (and thus starting salary) was recommended based on the contents of that résumé. Efforts to be concise and to highlight the experience, knowledge, and skills most relevant to that specific job may have downplayed or eliminated elements that were relevant to considerations for rank. In addition, the faculty committee making the rank recommendation may have found it more difficult to find those elements in the unfamiliar format. Similar scenarios may be true in any type of library where one might be hired at various ranks depending on qualifications. Efforts to present yourself appropriately could literally pay off.

Component parts of the résumé and curriculum vitae

Education

Placement of educational credentials is a clear area of differentiation between résumé and CV. Education is always listed on the first page of the CV as one of the first elements beneath the librarian's name and contact information. Placement of education in the résumé is more a matter of judgment and preference. For a newly degreed librarian, it should be placed at the beginning. This holds true for those with little experience, too. However, once the librarian has a few years of professional librarian experience, education may be moved after experience. In both document types, education is an appropriate section heading for this portion.

In the case of our real-world example (located in Appendix B), Tina's 2018 CV listed her education as one of the first elements on the top of the first page. In contrast, her 2015 résumé listed that same education as the very last element. Tina had more than 20 years of relevant professional experience since obtaining her Master of Library Science degree and she wanted to present that experience first because it was strongly relevant to the job ad. Making your strongest selling points highly visible reflects the reality that people sometimes skim rather than read closely. It's a valid choice for a résumé, but that order of presentation is not traditional for a CV.

The MLS/MLIS degree-granting institution and the year of the degree are important. Librarian job ads in the United States and Canada often specify an American Library Association (ALA) accredited MLS/MLIS as required, sometimes allowing an equivalent foreign degree. ALA maintains a historical list of accredited institutions online (American Library Association, 2019). Providing institution and graduation year enables the interviewers to verify that the degree-granting institution was accredited for that time period. You may prefer to omit your graduation date and only supply it if required.

Additional degrees and certifications, if current and relevant to the position, should also be listed in the "Education" section. Be sure to spell out any acronyms at the first use.

Grade point average (GPA), focus of coursework, membership in honor societies, and other degree-related information typically seem less and less important as the librarian gains relevant professional experience. You can choose for yourself whether or not to retain them as you update your documents over time.

Professional experience

The presentation of professional experience is similar in résumés and CVs. For comparison, see Tina's experience at "Small University," first in her 2015 résumé (used to apply to the university) and next in her 2018 CV (used to apply for promotion at the university in 2018.) On the résumé, Tina labelled this portion of the content as "Experience." On the CV, she used the heading "Performance of Professional Responsibilities," which is the phrase commonly used at her current institution. Apart from the updated grouping, the lists are mostly the same.

The significant differences between the two involve distinguishing "service" activities from professional experience. In the résumé, Tina includes serving on search committees and a faculty development committee as well as sponsoring a student group in her professional responsibilities. In her 2018 CV, those activities are moved to the "Service" area, which we'll address next.

Service

One of the trickier terms to consider in the realm of librarian jobs is "service." Service can describe numerous, overlapping concepts. It's important to understand the distinction.

The most obvious concept of service is providing service to patrons, such as doing reference work. In order to untangle the various meanings of the term, let's tease out how this use of the term differs from the academic use – even though Public Services, Reference Services, and Technical Services are certainly phrases used in the academic library world. We'll use reference or public service as the example because those are the areas where one most often directly interacts with patrons to provide a service. Providing reference "service" in the sense of giving assistance with informational and research inquiries falls into the category of "Professional Experience" or "Professional Responsibilities." That is, these are the responsibilities that would be listed first in a job ad for a reference or public services librarian. The academic library definition of "service" includes activities that are *outside* of this. Let's dig in further.

This second concept of service is helping or leading events and activities that aren't strictly job-related. Examples include volunteering with the state library association, helping the Friends group with their after-hours event or organizing a social media group to connect and share ideas with colleagues in similar positions at other institutions. These activities may or may not be required elements in the librarian's job and likewise may or may not be a rated element in the annual evaluation. An additional complexity is that some of these examples may be considered "Professional Development" rather than "Service." More on that a bit later.

In faculty-ranked academic positions, "service" overlaps with the activities mentioned above. However, it is defined in specific categories according to scope and type of activity, allocated a percentage of the librarian's work time, and evaluated in the annual review and during the promotion process. From the University of Central Florida (UCF) Libraries' Professional Activities Appropriate To Rank (PAAR) document, a guide for librarians seeking to rise to the next rank: "Service extends professional or discipline related contributions to the Libraries, University, and local, state, national, and international communities" (2006). At the authors' current institution, service activities at the libraries might include helping with Open Access Week activities or serving on the committee that selects the library employee of the year.

At the broader university level, service might include serving on a search committee for teaching faculty (i.e. outside the library) or serving (that word again!) on the Faculty Senate. Service at the local, state, national, and international levels usually involves library associations and groups, such as being on committees.

Service is expected to broaden in scope and audience as the librarian advances in rank and years of experience. An entry level librarian might contribute news items to the state library association's newsletter. At a higher level, the expectation might include serving in an elected leadership role for a national or international library association. A long-term commitment is more meaningful than a "one and done." Impact on more people or a deeper level of impact are also more meaningful.

Of course, academic institutions have a variety of requirements and expectations for librarians. The most apparent is likely whether librarians are classified as staff or faculty, and if faculty, whether they are tenure-track or not. An additional distinctive element is the type of higher education. Two-year institutions, commonly called community colleges in the United States, often differ in requirements and expectations from those granting bachelor's, master's, and Ph.D. degrees.

At the small community college, Sara found that service to the college was expected. Service to the community was nominal. Service to the library was almost a contradiction in term because the small staff necessitated all hands on-deck for nearly all events and programs and the concept of service implies something voluntary. Service to the profession wasn't valued by the college administration. It was valued by the library administration but funding for conference attendance was very limited so the support took the form of guidance and mentoring. Professional development and research and creative activities weren't part of the evaluation process.

Another distinction to make is the difference between attendance and involvement. There are many variations of the saying that a high percentage of success is showing up. However, simply attending a variety of events doesn't necessarily count. One must assume some measure of responsibility in order to claim credit. Attending a webinar to update one's cataloging skills is appropriate for mention in the professional development section as evidence of maintaining and growing the skillset. Attending a conference is also applicable for professional development. Actively serving on a committee, organizing a panel talk, doing a presentation, or otherwise sharing of your time and knowledge in a profession-related activity goes beyond passive learning or listening.

Shelly experienced the sometimes confusing and variable definitions of "service." She encountered several versions: volunteering in another library, "doing something directly for the profession [and] representing the profession in the larger community." A broad range of activities are encompassed by the one concept. Get clarification as needed.

Service is a specific element of the academic CV. It is often listed on the résumé under different guises. The following activities, listed under experience on Tina's résumé, were moved to a "Service" section on her CV:

- Chaired numerous search committees
- Sponsor (i.e. advisor) for student group
- Faculty development committee member.

Other broad service examples from the Professional Activities Appropriate to Rank document are listed below (2018). Depending on the relationship to one's core job duties, they could be listed under experience on a résumé or might be more suited for "Professional Activities," i.e. activities related to the profession but not to one's specific job.

- Library or institutional committees (appointed or elected)
- Serve as faculty advisor for student group
- Guest lecturer at local organizations, university classes or events (if not part of assigned job duties)
- Teach a for-credit course
- Serve as a consultant or expert in their area of expertise locally or nationally, such as to another library or library group.

Attending sporting and social events may be good for meeting people, networking, and "being seen" but aren't applicable for the résumé or CV.

Research and creative works or publications and presentations

On a CV, this section includes an array of activities generally predicated on making a contribution to the professional body of knowledge. These include articles and case studies published in scholarly journals, books, and book chapters. This category also includes doing presentations, posters, workshops, and panel discussions at conferences or webinars. Brief publications such as news items or reports of conference presentations are usually considered to be service. Short book reviews may also be service while longer, analytical reviews may fall into the research and creative category. Likewise with bibliographies.

Tina did have a separate "Publication" section on her résumé, recognizing that publishing an article in a peer-reviewed journal is worth drawing attention to. However, she lumped her presentations in with numerous other elements as we'll see in the next section.

Professional activities and professional memberships

On her résumé, Tina included her professional memberships (e.g. ALA), conference attendance, conference presentations, library association volunteer work, and continuing education activities all under an umbrella "Professional Activities" section. In retrospect, this seems like too many categories lumped together. If she were to need a résumé in the future, Tina would choose to have separate sections for Professional Memberships, Publications and Presentations, Professional Development (or Continuing Education), and Service/Library Association Activities. The distinctions would make for easier reading, likely without adding much space to the document.

Professional development and training (a.k.a. continuing education)

This section is generally a listing of how the librarian has kept their skills and knowledge up to date. It may encompass training sessions, webinars, courses, workshops, and such. An exhaustive list isn't necessary; a thematic grouping of topics is likely sufficient. Call out specific courses that are highly relevant to the job sought. Older or outdated coursework can be omitted or consolidated.

Awards and honors

Tina had one award on her résumé: a scholarship to a state library association conference. A few years later, she opted to skip an award section in her CV; by then the award was ten years old and represented a relatively small achievement. This was a judgment call: a more recent award, one with a national or international scope, or multiple awards would likely have merited an award section. These judgment calls can feel tricky. Age, scope, and applicability to current situation are all measures to consider.

Customize for each job application

You likely recognize that you need to apply for each position with the correct type of document. It's also important to hone your résumé or CV for each new application. Make sure your most relevant knowledge and experience is highlighted. If it's valid, move those bullet points up higher in the list. For instance, if your current job is 30% each reference, programming, and community engagement, and you plan to apply for a job that will really draw on your programming experience, then list that first. Then elevate community engagement if you apply for a job in that arena. Edit the wording to match the job ad if possible. For example, if you have done process-improvement work in your current job, and the job ad refers to workflow analysis, then consider if you can use the job ad phrasing instead. Look for ways to include the greater amount of information about highly relevant experience and be more concise about the less relevant. For example, if you're a teen librarian in a public applying for a first-year-experience librarian position at an academic, showcase your experience working with older teens and be more succinct in describing work with younger ones.

The cover letter

The authors heard from multiple librarians with hiring responsibilities that it is critical to include a cover letter with your application even if it's not listed as being required. The cover letter should explain how you meet the minimum job requirements in the ad. Many institutions require each candidate to meet those minimum requirements in order to advance in the process. Otherwise, the application ends there. The person screening the applications must be able to judge that the requirements are met. This screener may not be a librarian and/or may have little knowledge of different library environments. Furthermore, job titles and responsibilities vary greatly between libraries. Make sure the screeners judge in your favor by pointing out clearly how you meet each requirement.

Kathy, a university library director in the United States, said that documenting how you meet the minimum requirements is

> doubly important for librarians moving from one type of library to another. I have seen this done well in a variety of ways including bullet lists, tables with qualifications on one side and their experience/coursework on the other side, narrative paragraphs, etc. This should not just be a restatement of what is in their CV (unless buried in the CV). For example, teaching experience as a qualification could be addressed by public librarians as offering programming or even doing a story time with a line about literacy instruction or something else. Ability to meet the standards for promotion and tenure could be addressed by stating that they have an interest in researching XX or they have developed and

delivered a presentation at XX or they did extensive research in XX as a graduate student.

Kathy offered a specific example from her library where librarians are tenure-track. Her main concern in hiring from outside academia is the requirement to do scholarship and publication because people from other types don't always know enough about that to "even begin to ask good questions." One of the requirements to move past the initial screening of applications is to have something that supports tenure research and publication. The university library is careful not to hire librarians that they think will struggle in the tenure and promotion process. The librarian must demonstrate ideas about what they might want to research. Furthermore, the librarian will hopefully have some experience with research and publishing, even a newsletter or a presentation that they developed. Because this is a minimum requirement, any relevant experience must be pointed out in the cover letter. Do not expect whoever is doing the initial application review to hunt through your application for some mention of writing, research, or presenting. What seems obvious to you may not to them. While this is critical for tenure-track positions, it's also relevant to non-tenured university librarians who have job requirements for research and creative activities.

It's easy for people to fall into the trap of assuming that the work they have done is obvious because it is their day-to-day reality. But you must look at your application documents with fresh eyes and try not to assume that others know what you know; people in a different environment might not understand or even be aware of a process or program that is a common phenomenon in your world. The hiring librarian or human resources screener may have no experience with other types of libraries. Thus, it's up to the job applicant to spell out why their experience is relevant and meaningful.

Yolande, director of a countywide public library, spoke about cover letters and application materials: "I'm only going to see what you've presented to me." She said that many candidates only fill out the county's online application. They don't attach a résumé or cover letter, which limits what they can communicate to her. The cover letter (and résumé to some degree) are where the candidates can show her, the library director, what they've done in relation to the job. It's especially important for students and new graduates without much work experience and for those transitioning from a different environment to spell out all these skills and experiences that they've had and how those relate to the job ad.

The cover letter is also your chance to highlight experience that benefits from a bit of explanation. For example, when Sara applied for jobs that required supervisory experience, she used her cover letter to point out two things that didn't fit well in her résumé because they occurred infrequently. First, she discussed her library director appointing her "in charge" when the director was out of the office for multiple days. This involved resolving issues and making decisions for the library. Second, Sara was given a temporary assignment as supervisor of the student assistants, in addition to her other duties. In the course of this, Sara devised an efficient system to track the students' assigned tasks without constant monitoring. Via the cover letter, Sara highlighted to the search committee that she had supervision experience and had dealt with workflow and accountability issues, even though these weren't part of her regular responsibilities.

The moral of the story: don't let people draw their own conclusions about you and your abilities and experiences because those conclusions might not work to your advantage. Spell out what you can do and have done so that a stranger with no knowledge of your current environment can understand your qualifications.

Customize the cover letter to each job

It may be tempting to create one, generic cover letter and use it for every job application. This shortchanges you, however. The cover letter is the applicant's chance to speak directly to the person or committee who might hire you, to the person who might be your future boss. Why pass up the opportunity to tell them why you would be great for the job? Take those few minutes of their individual attention and use it to your best advantage with a cover letter crafted to that specific job and that specific library. We know it can be difficult to figure out how to do this, so we included several cover letters from Tina's 2014–2015 search below. Note that there is a common structure, but the specifics have been customized to each job. Also note that Tina found something about each job and library to express enthusiasm about. All of these comments were genuine; each situation had its own appeal, even if very different from one other.

Examples of customized cover letters

Note that the letters have been edited to use descriptive terms rather than the institution names. This helps differentiate the target institutions without the need for the reader to do internet research. It also shields some institutions who I decided not to pursue further.

For a Content Management Librarian at an elite, small private college:

I am pleased to apply for the position of Content Services Librarian at Elite Small College. I think that my experience and skills are a good fit for the job.

After eight years at Small University Library, I am ready for new challenges. I would welcome the opportunity to work at a well-respected, service-oriented college like Elite Small College, and to return to the Northeast.

I have broad-based technical services skills, as well as years of experience in providing research assistance and library instruction. My cataloging experience covers both copy and original cataloging for physical and electronic materials in many formats. I also have experience with numerous acquisitions models, from purchasing and leasing to demand-driven. Collaborating with public services to present materials in an attractive and discoverable manner is also a priority.

Working closely with my technical services colleagues at Small University, I have helped transition the library's collection from mostly print and physical media to primarily electronic resources, greatly improving access via an emphasis on multi-user content. We have also transitioned from generally using traditional library vendors to heavily incorporating newer sources, like Amazon, which can allow us to put requested materials into our patrons' hands in just a few days. My goal is always to obtain materials for our patrons quickly, in the most cost-effective way, and to enable discovery with a robust description.

I most enjoy working in small institutions with the kind of fast-paced, dynamic, student-centered environment that your job ad describes. I am a self-starter, love to solve puzzles, and am eager to grow, as well as bringing a lot of applicable experience to the table. In short, I think I have a lot to offer the library and the college and I would welcome the chance to discuss this with you.

Sincerely,

For a Library Technical Services Manager position at Midsize Western City

To the Hiring Committee,

I am excited to apply for the position of Library Technical Services Manager. I think my experience and skills are a good match for the job, as I am well-versed in providing user-centered technical services and collaborating with colleagues to continually improve library services.

With responsibility for the entire collection budget, I currently manage acquisitions, cataloging, and processing of monographs (traditional and electronic) at Small University Library. For the last five months, I have also been the interim Electronic and Continuing Resources Librarian, managing all aspects of our databases, serials, and EBSCO Discovery layer. I am also involved in collection management, collaborating closely with our Collection Development Librarian to assess collection needs and plan future directions. We evaluate cost, use, bibliographic, and community metrics to build an efficient, data-driven collection.

In addition, I have extensive experience with various ILSs, most recently Brand XYZ Integrated Library System. I work heavily with its technical services functions and their intersection with public services functions. As a resource person for library staff, I troubleshoot a variety of issues and help others learn the system. I have also participated in pre- or post-migration work in several libraries. For example, at Big City Public Library, I trained the cataloging staff on SIRSI Workflows and wrote the unit manual on the system.

Providing the best possible service to our community is always my priority. For instance, I have transitioned most purchasing of container-based patron-requests to Amazon. This generally allows us to put requests in our patrons' hands within days, unlike the weeks or months it can take with traditional library vendors.

Streamlined and efficient technical services processes are part of providing good service, so I am always alert for opportunities to improve. For example, I recently overhauled the workflow for our print standing orders, reducing the necessary expertise needed and thereby broadening the pool of personnel who can handle them.

During my career I have supervised from one to four staff, and had the responsibility for training, directing, and orienting many others, as well as creating and updating policies, procedures, and workflows. I am a proven team leader in my current institution, chairing numerous search committees (including two in the last six months) and leading the ILS/LSP Team in seeking our next automation system.

After eight years at a university, I am ready for new challenges and want to return to public library work. Your job ad calls for an innovative, collaborative, and service-oriented person; this describes me very well. I hope to have the chance to discuss this with you.

Sincerely,

For a large public university Head of Cataloging and Metadata Services position

Dear Search Committee,

I am excited to apply for the position of Head of Cataloging and Metadata Services at Large Public University. After eight years at Small University Library, I am ready for new challenges and am eager to move into a position specializing in cataloging and metadata services. I have broad-based technical services skills, including original cataloging of materials in numerous formats using AACR2/RDA, MARC21, and LC and Dewey classification; database maintenance; quality control; and creating policies, procedures, and workflows.

Our ILS is Brand XYZ Integrated Library System, and I work extensively with its technical services functions. I am solely responsible for all load-profiling, and load vendor records for multiple e-book and streaming-video collections, as well as OCLC records for traditional materials. As a resource person for the library staff, I troubleshoot a variety of issues and help others learn to utilize Brand XYZ.

Working collaboratively and creating connections between functional units is the norm for me. I work closely and frequently with our Collection Development Librarian and Electronic and Continuing Resources Librarian to maximize discoverability of our resources. As my current duties include acquisitions, I am well-versed in incorporating new acquisitions methods (such as demand-driven) into the technical services workflow. I have also worked with our archivists on several trials for digital projects.

Regarding my experience with non-MARC metadata, I was a beta-tester for III's digital asset management tool, ContentPro (Dublin Core) and I have cross-walked data between various formats, using both OCLC Connexion and MarcEdit, as well as manually, for several trial projects, mostly involving archival collections. I readily learn new standards and technologies and would welcome the chance to be more involved in non-MARC formats.

I have supervised personnel in most of my positions, and have led numerous teams, such as our next-gen ILS/LSP exploratory task force and two search committees just in the past year.

Your job ad calls for a collaborative, creative, and transformative librarian. This describes me very well. I think my experience and skills are a good fit for the job, and I hope to have the chance to discuss this with you.

Sincerely,

For a Head of Collection Services position at a Small Midwestern City

Dear Mr. Library Director,

I am pleased to apply for the position of Head of Collection Services at the Small Midwestern City Public Library.

After eight years at Small University Library, I would welcome the opportunity to return to public library work and to serve a wider community. I have broad-based technical services skills including collection management, acquisitions and budgeting, cataloging and classification, processing, stacks maintenance, data analysis, and working with vendors.

In addition, I have extensive experience with Integrated Library System (which I understand to be a close cousin to Brand XYZ), working heavily with its technical services functions and their intersection with public services functions. As a resource person for library staff, I troubleshoot a variety of issues and help others learn the system. I also make frequent use of MarcEdit and readily learn software programs as needed to improve and enhance the workflow.

I work closely with my colleagues to create an appealing collection for our community as cost-effectively as possible, based on patron needs, requests, and use patterns. While the academic library collection is predominantly scholarly, we also have substantial popular collections of books, magazines, and DVDs, designed to encourage frequent visits. We also try hard to delight our patrons with good service, such as quick turn-around time for purchase requests.

Having provided reference assistance or customer service in most of my positions, I am experienced at creating positive patron interactions. I have also delivered many research instruction sessions to students, as well as presentations to professional groups, and so would be comfortable speaking with community groups and civic meetings.

I am ready for new challenges and I would be glad to relocate to Small Midwestern City, to be closer to old friends and family. I think my experience and skills are a good fit for the job and I hope to have the chance to discuss this with you.

Sincerely,

For Electronic Resources Librarian at the Very Large University

Dear Search Committee,

I am excited to apply for the position of Electronic Resources Librarian at Very Large University. After several years of intensively building the electronic collections at Small University, I am eager to move into a position specializing in e-resources.

As the Acquisitions and Metadata Librarian at Small University, I collaborated closely with our Collection Development Librarian to create the most current and extensive monographic collection ever available to our community. We added six new e-book platforms, increasing the number of titles by over 400%, including a large DDA collection. We also established the library's first streaming video collection, including both DDA and subscription packages, as well as the first article-on-demand package. Extending my e-resources experience, I was the interim Electronic and Continuing Resources Librarian at Small University for five months in 2014. I troubleshot access problems; managed renewals, new subscriptions, and licensing questions; and updated serials bibliographic and holdings data.

I also have experience with Discovery Layer, having been part of the implementation team as well as the ongoing management. We have made every effort to make Discovery Layer patron-friendly, from meaningful labels on limiters to frequent catalog updates. We are also examining the impact on statistics, and the implications for resources that either don't partner with EBSCO or don't display well in the context of discovery.

Having cataloged for many years, I am familiar with AACR2, RDA, and FRBR. I am also responsible for all bibliographic maintenance and enhancement work in my current position. Much of my bibliographic work currently involves batch-loading and batch-editing of vendor record sets, to provide the richest possible data for ingestion into our discovery layer.

I have extensive experience with Integrated Library System, working heavily with its technical services functions and their intersection with public services functions. As a resource person for library staff, I troubleshoot a variety of issues and help others learn the system.

My small technical services team is responsible for nearly all aspects of providing our community with the best possible collection and access to that collection. In order to do so, we must function well as a team: collaborating, solving problems, and seeking new opportunities to improve. Furthermore, I have been part of two such high-functioning technical services teams, as all three of my current TS co-workers have been in their jobs for less than a year.

Workflow analysis is an ongoing part of my job. For instance, I created workflows for new demand-driven acquisitions models, and for efficiently adding and updating tens of thousands of MARC records into our database. I continue to adjust and improve those workflows as vendor options change and as DDA has become a normal acquisitions method.

I am collaborative, analytical, love to solve problems, and function well in a cross-departmental, multi-cultural environment. In short, I think my skills and experience are a good fit for your job, and I would be very pleased to have the chance to discuss this with you.

Sincerely,

The interview

Ready for true confessions? Tina walked into her very first academic library interview with not-a-clue about where the library fit in the structure of the university, the ways that academic libraries differed from publics, or even what a provost was. The latter was a bit awkward when she was walked across campus for an interview with said provost whom she took to be a human-resources figure. The internet was around in those days, she knew people who worked in academic libraries, and so she has no explanation for why she entered the situation so clueless about the environment – she had focused solely on preparation to talk about any aspect of technical services, which was the job's focus. But the broader environment or how the interview experience would differ from that at a public library? Nope! Tina didn't know what she didn't know and neither did anyone on the search committee who might have been able to clue her in as the day progressed. So, let's make sure you don't make the same mistakes.

Who will the candidate interact with?

The differences begin with the personnel who organize and lead the search process. The public library process will likely be initiated and lead by the municipality human resources department in conjunction with the library director or the manager of the department with the vacancy. Academic interviews are usually initiated and led by a search committee made up of librarians and library staff. Our interviewees have generally stated that interviews with school districts will be with a panel of interviewers (such as the school principal(s) and school board members) as will academic library interviews and larger public libraries. Smaller publics may be a one-person interview with the library director. If a panel interview would make you more nervous, then consider rehearsing techniques to diffuse that, such as making eye contact with whomever is asking a question and responding to them as an individual before turning your attention to the next questioner.

If you're given an interview-day agenda with the names of those you will be meeting, you'll obviously want to look all those people up. If you aren't given that information, try to ascertain who is in the position's reporting chain and look those people up. For instance, if you're interviewing for a university technical services job, find out the name of the highest ranked librarian related to technical services; find out who the library dean/director is; and, if possible, figure out who the dean/director reports to (probably a provost or vice president). If you're applying to a school system, learn who is on the school board.

Length of interview day

Brian advised:

> keep your expectations kind of loose. [Don't] be attached to any particular kind of structure or format of the interview, and the stuff you see online in terms of what an academic interview is going to be like ... it's just guidance ... it doesn't mean it's actually going to happen that way.

Academic library interviews may last a full day or longer. You may have dinner the night before with one or more members of the search committee and/or someone in the position's reporting chain. The interview day will likely consist of many parts: a presentation on a designated topic, and interviews with the search committee, the position's supervisor, the library director or dean, and the position's department or unit. Expect lunch and a coffee or break with potential colleagues or direct reports. You will likely be taken on a tour of the library and at least part of the campus. However, this is not uniformly applied. One interviewee told us about a university library interview that lasted a total of one hour.

At community colleges, the interview experience can vary greatly. Our interviewees related stories of interviews lasting anywhere from one to four hours at various community (i.e. two year) colleges.

Public library interviews are usually much shorter, typically two or three hours. Expect interviews with a group of librarians and staff, the library director or the position's immediate supervisor, and a tour of the library. There may be a meeting with the position's direct report if applicable. Shared meals are unusual. This is similar to the experience our interviewees had at special and governmental libraries. We were also told about corporate library "interviews" that were really more conversations with the potential boss and perhaps a colleague. Once the right "fit" was determined, the job was offered on the spot.

Whether travel was paid for

In the authors' experience, academic libraries pay for airfare, hotel, and transportation to and from the airport during the interview process while public libraries generally do not. Of course, this will vary between institutions as well as by position. If you're applying to an administrative or other high-level job, you may be "wined and dined," so to speak.

Required to do a presentation

Academics almost always require the candidate to give a presentation on a topic related to the job as part of the interview day. A PowerPoint-type visual component is usually an element of this but it's best to verify what is expected and what kind of audio-visual/computer equipment will be available to you. Expect a question and answer session following your presentation. We haven't heard of presentations being the norm at any other type of environment.

Screening materials required pre-interview

It is becoming more common for public libraries to require some kind of additional submission prior to being selected to interview. These submissions may take the place of phone or video interviews. This typically comes in the form of an email from the municipality human resources department. Some examples include: recording a one-minute video response to each of five or six questions; submitting a collection development proposal to address a specific scenario; providing written answers to five to ten questions that might be typical phone-interview material.

Tina encountered several of these exercises in her job hunt and was left with a strong opinion: the value of these screening techniques (which likely require less personnel time than an interview on the library's end) is understandable. However, they gave her a sense of being asked for a lot of effort without being given anything in return. When you do a phone or in-person interview, you meet people, have the opportunity to ask questions, and otherwise size up the interviewers while they're doing the same to you. With the online submissions, you give but you get nothing beyond the intellectual exercise. Of course, if you want or need the job, do the work. We recommend keeping copies of anything you submit in case it can be re-used.

Preparing for the interview in a different library environment

As you might expect of a group of librarians, our interviewees highly recommended doing your research. Explore the website of both the library and the overarching institution. Search for local news sources. Find out what the hot issues are in that kind of library. For instance, Fred gave the example of the current trend of social workers being hired in some public libraries to assist patrons who are at risk. This will allow you to ask questions that demonstrate your understanding of the library and its broader context. Brian related the experience of being on a hiring committee for a library in the midst of much-publicized budget cuts. Interviewees who only asked about academic freedom and publishing opportunities – and never referred to the budget situation – seemed unprepared.

Email lists and library forums such as ALA Connect can help with learning the hot-topic areas. Search the names of the library director or other names associated with the library. Do they have a current LinkedIn profile or other listing of their current professional associations? Look at the websites of the relevant associations, committees, etc. to see what they're up to.

Talk with any friends who work or have worked in that type of library (if they've worked in that specific environment, all the better.) Librarians tend to be happy to share information. Search online for "working in X library type." You might learn of a relevant association or newsletter. Consider informal social media, too, such as local Facebook or Meetup groups.

Our interviewees also recommend learning what the other library is doing and what the goals are. Then figure out how your characteristics and experience transfer to that role. Brian says

> people don't always understand what librarians are doing in different kinds of settings and you just have to be careful to sell yourself and indicate how what you're doing is similar to what people are doing [in the destination environment].

You may need to directly address biased perceptions of librarians in your current environment. Jodie found that public librarians sometimes thought that school librarians had a purely teaching role and didn't know library skills. She had to explicitly relate her collection development, cataloging, and programming experience in order to successfully make her case for a public library job.

If there are preferred qualifications on the job ad with which you aren't familiar, Shelly advised to "try and get some training or some education that would give [you] something to say in an interview – to say 'yes, I understand this even if I haven't worked with it.'" This could mean watching a webinar or recorded conference presentation online or reading an article or blogpost about the topic. This also gives you fodder for asking the interviewer(s) about how the process is done at that library. With background knowledge, you can ask better questions.

Marian advised acknowledging what you need to learn for the new job and stating how you will correct those shortcomings. She gave the example of needing to learn how public library funding worked in that area and the applicable state and municipal laws. She cited the network of public librarian friends in the state who were willing to mentor her.

Think about how your experience relates to the job requirements. Plan to connect these explicitly for the interviewers. With her school library background, Marian needed to show that her experience was relevant to the public library she interviewed with. Marian explained that her proposals to the school board contained the same elements as proposals to the village council. Each needed to contain funding information, project justification, and background information. This demonstrated a highly relevant experience in a different library environment.

Many interviewees advised remembering what all libraries have in common. Marian cited the following: being aware of the needs of the user, principles such as freedom of information and freedom to read, the collection development process, and knowing good reference sources for various kinds of information requests. Can you draw parallels based on these commonalities?

Contextualize your past work for your present situation

You can likely find parallels between the work you've done and what is required for a new position. This helps the interviewer understand what you've done and how relevant it is to their needs. Here are examples from our interviewees of contextualizing their experience to fit the requirements of a new environment:

- Helping bookstore customers find something to read relates to doing book talks at the public library
- Teaching basic cataloging skills to small town librarians at a multi-type library organization relates to doing instruction at an academic library
- Budget reports and requests to a school board from a school librarian relates to budget reports and requests to a municipal library board from a library director or CEO
- Relating the schools or colleges within a university to branches within a public library system, each having their own primary clientele, interests and demands, and unique situation within the larger organization.
- Managing a statewide purchasing cooperative for a multi-type resource center relates to working with group purchasing models at an academic.

There are many examples where the scope of an activity varies between a large versus small library but the concerns and processes will be sufficiently similar to give plenty of common ground for relating your experience. When Tina was working at a big city's public library system, she applied to work at a small academic. She had strong experience with ILS implementations; staff training; and process improvement, all of which strongly correlated to the academic library's needs.

- Managing a discovery layer
- Analyzing collection usage
- Loading bibliographic records for electronic resource packages or databases
- Preparing for and going through an ILS migration
- Planning programs
- Teaching information literacy or searching skills
- Training staff
- Interacting with patrons who are at risk or otherwise challenging
- Being comfortable and friendly when interacting with the public

Be clear about the scope at which you have worked because that's not obvious. Put a number on how many people report to you; what size budget you manage; how many programs or instruction sessions you coordinate each year, etc. These numbers don't always correlate to the size of the institution and may work in your favor.

Finally, maybe you have relevant skills that come from outside your library job. Yolande, a public library system director, says that customer service experience is needed for many jobs. If your work experience is purely back-office with little to no customer interaction, then look to other parts of your life for relevant experience, such as volunteering. Yolande gave the example of a cataloger who volunteered reading to children at a story-time. Tina volunteered for a non-library organization, editing and publishing their weekly newsletter. The task necessitated learning the MailChimp marketing software's free version, which became another skill for her to list on a résumé or CV. This sort of skill could be translated to a library without a full-time public relations person but needing to keep in touch with patrons, Friends groups, or other constituencies. What are you doing with your free time that might translate to a beneficial line on your job application?

Benefit of interviewing a lot

Sometimes the job candidate and the right job find each other quickly and the job search ends after little hunting. But sometimes it takes longer and that isn't always a bad thing. Here's Tina's experience:

> People are surprised when I tell them I interviewed for a dozen or more jobs before I accepted my current position. Obviously, sometimes I wasn't

the chosen candidate. Several times, I learned something about the job that was unappealing and I withdrew. But the surprising thing was that my understanding of what I wanted evolved as I went through my search. My first Skype interview was with an institution that was a much larger version of the one that I was ready to leave, and the job mostly mirrored the one I had. They invited me to an in-person interview and of course that feels great. But I declined and withdrew from that search. Reflecting on the commonalities that I noticed during the Skype interview helped me recognize that I wanted a bigger change. That realization opened my mind to other job postings – I had only been noticing ones for jobs similar to what I had already done, but afterwards I started looking at postings that seemed like more of a stretch.

The benefits of going on numerous interviews include: practice preparing for and answering interview questions; practice in questioning interviewers and assessing the answers; improved skills in researching libraries, their governing bodies, and potential colleagues; it becomes easier to accept rejections when there are other applications in the hopper or other interviews scheduled; customizing the cover letter and résumé for each position gives one a flexible understanding of their skills and experience and improves the ability to draw parallels between past experience and the job ad. Brian echoes the benefit of experience in interviewing: "as I have been interviewing throughout the year I've gotten better and better at making that sales pitch."

How does it feel?

Lots of interviews also gives the candidate many opportunities to see what different library environments are like and assess how you as an individual are treated.

- "Between interviews at this one public library, I was sent on break alone at the coffeeshop in the basement, which felt very inhospitable," said one librarian. "The excuse was that librarians leave early on Fridays in the summer. But if you have a candidate pay their own way to fly in and stay in a hotel, one or two people could take 15 minutes to chat during the break."
- Are people friendly and engaged with you? Or are you shuttled from one encounter to another like a commodity?
- Are they considerate of your needs, such as offering water or a restroom break?
- Are you given a tour of the building or campus and shown where your office/desk would be? Tina became leery of a position when she was given a tour of the whole library, except for the department that she had applied to.

- Do you have time to ask questions of people in close proximity to the position, such as direct reports and departmental peers?
- In group meetings, do people seem comfortable with each other? Is there friendly chatter between colleagues?
- What do interviewers say about the job? Tina had an uncomfortable interview with a director who wanted a candidate to fulfill numerous roles with no relationship to the job ad.
- What do interviewers say about themselves? We heard about an interview with a library director who said she was counting down the days until she retired.

A job application is just a request for more information

Several librarians said they had applied for jobs just to find out more about them. One said, "A job application is just a request for more information." If they were intrigued by what they learned, they continued with the process. You can withdraw your application at any point if you decide that the position isn't right for you. A phone or Skype interview can tell you about the culture of the place that advertised the job. We don't recommend applying for jobs that you have no intention of accepting if it gets to that point – you're wasting the time of many people involved in the process – but if you're genuinely open to the opportunity, then pursuing it is fine. Remember that you have a choice about whether to proceed at each step.

Comfort for disappointing outcomes

Sometimes, you can put in a great application and do a great interview and still not get the job. There is a balancing act to perform when getting disappointing news after an application or interview.

First, consider honestly, but without beating yourself up, if there are things you could improve upon. Revisit this chapter and other sources of support to see if your application documents and interview skills could be bettered. In some cases, you may be able to get feedback from the library about why you weren't the chosen candidate. This isn't common – many are not allowed to due to fear of lawsuits – but it may be worth asking if you thought that job was a really good fit. Focus solely on the opportunity to learn and improve. Do not engage in self-recrimination. Be as kind to yourself as you would to a friend asking for support in their own job search.

Second, remember that the employer is looking for the best fit for their library. They may think your skills were wonderful but another candidate's were better. They may feel a different personality was a better fit. Other scenarios, such as internal candidates, can also come into play. There's another job out there for which you are the candidate with the best fit. Go forward and find that one.

Laying the groundwork

You may recall the reference to a state library association award that the recipient might have needed to document ten years after receipt, while working at another institution in a different state. The website of the award-granting institution didn't list past winners of their award, only the current one. Let's take that example to heart and discuss methods of tracking (and remembering) your career accomplishments.

One very useful tool to examine past versions of websites is "The Wayback Machine," a web service that can help in documenting past achievements that occurred during the internet age. The Wayback Machine is also called The Internet Archive and is located at https://archive.org/web/. It creates copies of webpages over time. If you can supply the relevant URL, you may be able to view a copy of a years-old website that has changed numerous times since. If you're fortunate, your achievement will have been archived when the site was crawled.

While assembling her promotion portfolio, Tina came to consider her career in terms of when the internet was widely in use and when it wasn't. The internet era provides more opportunity to track down details of your past work life but completeness of websites certainly varies. If your career spans pre- or early internet years, you may lack documentation for that time period, and it can be difficult to recover. Contacting an agency and asking for any documentation that they have is worth a try. Whether they will be willing or able to accommodate requests will, of course, vary. Likewise, colleagues from that era may have something to share.

Retain documentation such as appointment notifications, acknowledgments, and thank you notes from people who chaired committees on which you served, people you completed projects and presentations with, and similar. The program booklets or websites of conferences where you presented or volunteered, certificates of continuing education, and awards are other examples of documentation to keep, whether in paper or electronic. Come up with a simple organization technique (by committee, project, date, etc.) and keep these things safely filed away whether in print or digitally. Important documents on the work computer drives and paper files should be saved at home, too. These include performance reviews, notes of commendation or thanks, presentations, and publications.

People often rely on their work email account to track past career events. It's best to also keep a copy in your personal email, computer folders, or cloud storage. After a job ends, access to the work email account and contact list usually ends immediately. Forward emails documenting achievements to your personal email account and then file them away. Unfortunately, jobs can end suddenly, so it's best to document as you go.

Here is a simple method to track your accomplishments without undue effort. Create a text document in the application of your choice. Add brief,

Preparing for interviews and promotion 57

dated entries for any accomplishments and projects in chronological order. Create a calendar reminder or an appointment with yourself to update the document every week or two – and really do it. (If it's a document on your work computer, email or upload a back up to your personal email or online account occasionally or print a paper copy for home.) Once or twice a year, use the list to update your CV and/or résumé. Then you're ready if opportunity comes knocking. Conversely, if you find yourself unexpectedly on the hunt, you'll be so glad to be prepared.

Interviewee comments on interviewing

Marian explained her approach to interviewing at a different type of library:

> I think you also have to, if I'm going to interview, like when I came to interview for this [public library director] position, I had to acknowledge right out front that I was not a public librarian by experience, so that there would be things I'd have to learn, that I wouldn't know not having been in a public library before. Those things are around funding, around different kind of laws for the state, for the municipality, just different logistical pieces that public libraries have to think about that school libraries don't, that academic libraries don't. So, I had to acknowledge my shortcomings and talk about how I would fix them. Like I had to point out that I had an extensive network of colleagues in this state who were public librarians who were willing to mentor me. I just had to address that issue and how I was going to strengthen myself in that area of weakness. And I also had to talk about the things we had in common. I had done many a proposal for a school board that had to have all of the different pieces that we have to have for our village council here. So, when I do an item for the agenda for a council meeting, it's got all those same sorts of pieces. The funding information, the justification, the background, all that. It's all the same, I just had to talk about it that way, so that they could see that in fact I was doing the same sorts of functions, just for a different audience. So, those were the biggies for me; it's focusing on what is absolutely the same across all libraries and also acknowledging that some things are different, and I was going to have to learn that.

Maureen discussed how many people might be conducting an interview.

> Normally when you go to an interview for a school district or academic, you're looking at definitely a panel interview, whereas a lot of the individual [public] libraries here in Alberta, you're looking at one person doing the interview. Now, if it's a director or manager position, then you might have the whole board actually doing the interview.

Pam used her experience as a library science lecturer to sell herself during her interview for a position as an academic librarian.

> one of the arguments I put forward to move into this academic librarian role was that I had many years as an academic [i.e. teaching faculty], and so I could actually give [the librarians] the academic perspective … . Understanding where an academic is coming from when they say I want this journal article or I want this, I'm doing this research and I want you to provide resources to support that.

Lisa said,

> one of those things that can help the hiring committee look past the places you've worked is if they know who you are, and they know what your skills are. So, I mean, as an academic librarian it would be a lot easier for me to move into the public library if I knew who the public library people were in my town, for example, in my city. Or if I was on a similar association and worked with someone on a committee … or if I did a conference presentation or met someone at a conference.

Audrey said,

> I think probably it's more important for you to figure out if it's going to be a good fit, looking around, than it is to be worried about how you're coming across in an interview. I spent way too much time worrying and preparing answers to those lists of questions and practicing that, but I didn't spend nearly enough time thinking about what qualities the institution had put forward and what qualities I would put forward on a daily basis, and whether or not those would be a good mesh.

Jenn gave advice based on her experience as an interviewer:

> When I interview people now, we ask them questions that there's really no right or wrong answer to. It's really behavior-based and experience-based. Lots of "tell us about a time when you did X." "Tell us about a time when you worked as part of a team." I don't care that the team was successful or not; I don't care that the end game of the project was stellar. I care how you behaved in that situation and how you reacted to things.

Items for reflection or action

1. Knowing that you may have to pay for transportation costs for some library interviews, consider how much and how frequently you are willing and able to spend. What kinds of jobs and which locations would be worth the expenditure? Could you stay with friends or family?

2. Here are several common, generic interview questions. Start thinking through answers, and relevant stories that convey your knowledge and experience. Rehearse out loud until you can say your answer fluidly. Adjust answers according to the focus of each job (i.e. try to think of a collection-focused example when applying for a collection development job and an instruction/teaching anecdote for that kind of job). Being able to address these questions will be relevant in nearly any interview; while the exact wording of questions varies, these topics are typically covered.
    a. Why do you want this job? (Your answer needs to reflect aspects of the job. If you want to live in that location, that can be a secondary reason. If you need any job, you should still be able to respond to the question with appealing aspects of each job that you interview for. You may be in a survival situation, but you need to give the interviewers a reason to consider you a good candidate. Needing a paycheck is totally understandable but it doesn't demonstrate why you're a better choice than other interviewees in the same situation.)
    b. Why are you qualified to do this job? (This is your "elevator pitch" to sell yourself.)
    c. Greatest strength(s) and an example of how you have used it at work
    d. Biggest weakness(es) and an example of how you have worked to address it.
    e. Most relevant experience related to three to four elements of the job description
    f. What would your direct report and/or supervisor tell us about you?
    g. Tell us how you handled a project or task where you failed.
    h. How do you stay current in your area of the profession?
    i. What kind of working environment suits you best?
    j. How do you handle interpersonal conflict? Or What kind of colleague are you? Give an example.
3. Create a list of questions that you want to ask of the interviewers. This will vary somewhat from job to job but it's helpful to have a core list in mind, so you're not caught off guard in the moment. Having no questions to ask makes it sound like you're not that interested. Examples:
    a. What are you looking for in the person who takes this position? What are your priorities for the first year?
    b. What's your favorite/least favorite thing about working here?
    c. I noticed XX in the job ad/on your website/in a news article about the library and I'd like to hear more. Could you tell me about that? You mentioned Project Z, which this position will be involved in; could you tell me more about that?
    d. What's the communication style like (with library/institutional leadership or within the department, etc.)?
    e. With your future supervisor: what's your leadership or supervisory style? How do you see this position working with the rest of the team?

4. Is your CV or résumé up to date? Make sure significant items from your most recent review or from the past year's work are listed clearly. If you're thinking of applying for jobs in an environment that generally requires the other document, create that. Ask a trusted friend or colleague for feedback about format and clarity. Some conferences offer feedback for job-seekers' documents; typically, experienced librarians volunteer to provide input. In a similar vein, some library school alumni groups may offer this service by member volunteers to other members.

References

American Library Association. (2019) Accredited Library and Information Studies Master's Programs from 1925 through Present. Retrieved from www.ala.org/educationcareers/accreditedprograms/directory/historicallist

Internship and Career Center, University of California, Davis. (2018) *Resume vs. Curriculum Vitae: What's the Difference?* Retrieved from https://icc.ucdavis.edu/materials/resume/resumecv. Viewed January 13, 2019.

University of Central Florida Libraries. (2006). *Professional Activities Appropriate to Rank*. Internal UCF report. Unpublished.

Further reading

American Library Association New Members Round Table. *Resume Review Service Committee of New Members Round Table (NMRT)*. American Library Association. www.ala.org/rt/nmrt/oversightgroups/comm/resreview/resumereview

Franks, T. P., Budzise-Weaver, T., & Reynolds, L. J. (2017). Unlocking Library Search Committees at ARL Public Universities: Techniques and Best Practices for Getting Hired. *Information and Learning Science*, 118(5/6), 252–265. https://doi.org/10.1108/ILS-04-2017-0024

Hodge, M. & Spoor N. (2012). Congratulations! You've Landed an Interview. What Do Hiring Committees Really Want? *New Library World*, (3/4), 139. https://doi.org/10.1108/03074801211218534

4 Mentorship

Librarians moving to a new library will find themselves needing support. Mentors can provide emotional support as well as an outside perspective for librarians in transition. There are many ways to find those mentors, and many different types of mentors, from existing friendships to new relationships with industry leaders. Librarians will find there are many opportunities to connect with other librarians, from conferences and listservs to nearby colleagues. Once the connection has been made, the librarian should consider appropriate means of communication and questions to ask. Even in the midst of a big career change, librarians should still consider mentoring others, as sharing expertise is a vital component of the library profession. Meaningful connections can be made, even without ever meeting in person. The chapter includes discussion of different types of mentorships, such as formal versus informal, professional and career, institutional, conference, life coach or fan, community, peer mentors and support groups, and self-mentorship. The chapter offers tips for finding a mentor and becoming a mentor as well as a list of the qualities that matter in mentors. It concludes with a support system summary and questions for reflection.

Why you might want a mentor

Many librarians have mentors or had them in the past, though it's far from a universal experience. When you're about to undertake a career change, it's a good time to consider if you have a mentor option or to try to re-ignite an old relationship. Job changes can upend your traditional support base. That senior colleague you used to run ideas past isn't down the hall anymore. The mentor–mentee relationship can be one of the best sources of professional support. A mentor can help with career guidance and networking opportunities and provide a trusted opinion.

What kind of questions would you like to ask a mentor? Envisioning what you want to talk about might help point to what kind of mentor you want and where to look for them. Do you want to ask about career trajectory, and how they got to their current position? Do you have questions about your area of librarianship that you want help to contextualize or solve? Do you have an off-the-wall idea that you think could be potentially great? For a librarian going through a career transition, finding a mentor in the same type or size as your new library environment can be extremely helpful. You can benefit greatly from having someone you can ask "is this normal" type questions. For example, if you are new to public libraries and you have an experienced public librarian as a mentor, you can ask questions about fines: "Does every public library refuse to drop fines, or is this a unique situation?" Also consider if you want to be able to talk with someone in person or if online or phone calls acceptable or preferable to you.

Types of mentorship

Let's look at different types of mentorship. Our interviewees suggested variations on the traditional model, so we'll share many of their comments. While we discuss numerous types of mentors below, real life tends to blur categories. The same person may fulfill numerous categories for you. Some colleagues will slip in and out of a mentoring stance depending on the topic at hand.

Formal versus informal

The first distinction to make is between formal and informal mentoring relationships. The formal path typically means that a mentor and mentee are formally assigned to each other. Sometimes this is done by an external authority. For instance, within your institution, a senior colleague may be assigned to be your mentor when you start the job; or a mentor at another institution might be assigned to you if you both register for a mentorship program through a library association or another professional group. Sometimes a formal mentoring relationship is begun by one of the parties asking or suggesting that they begin such a dialogue. The formal mentorship is often the traditional model that people think of when the topic arises. But there are other options.

An informal mentorship develops organically. You work in the same library or participate in the same organization and become acquainted over time. If this is someone whose actions you admire and whose opinions you trust, and if you interact with them on a regular basis, a mentoring relationship may evolve. Research has found that these informal connections are quite highly valued. In a research article, James et al. found that the librarians they surveyed preferred the advice of their informal mentors over formal mentors, and even thought that their informal mentors had a better impact on their career (2015). So be creative in who you consider "adopting" as your mentor(s), and don't discount one type versus another.

Professional/career mentor

These are two closely related, somewhat overlapping concepts and you may have one person fulfill both roles. The professional mentor is the person you can ask all sorts of questions about your work, handling stress and staff, project management, and the nitty gritty of how to get your job done. This person probably works in the same area of the profession as you so they can advise you about topics such as skills to build, appropriate professional development opportunities, and ways to approach a difficult project or a difficult manager.

Ideally, a career mentor is someone who has the job you want to work your way up to. A career mentor is the person you talk to about your broader career plans. They can help you figure out your overall goals, what steps you can take now to prepare yourself, and whether a job advertisement sounds like a good fit for you. A career mentor could critique your résumé or CV or suggest that it's time to move on from a certain job. Of course, your career goals will evolve and change over time. You may have several career mentors over the course of your working life, or, indeed, several at one time for different aspects of your career (for example, one mentor for the job aspect of your career and another to help with your publishing or writing goals).

Anna found a career mentor early on and remains in contact with him.

> I was really lucky in my first post, I identified Matthew, who's a friend. He was my line manager really briefly, and one of the things I realized was that our management styles were really different, and Matthew approaches things in a way that I would never have thought to approach things. I can be quite – you know there's a confrontation index, how many things you'd raise and how many things you'd leave – and my confrontation index is quite high, and Matthew's is quite low. And yet, he's a very effective manager, and I'm a very effective manager in different ways. So, I identified him, and I did formally ask him to be my mentor. I talk to him, when jobs come up, he reads job adverts, when I've had issues trying to go through things like management change and restructures, I try to talk to him about those issues. We meet a couple of times a year.

Being a good career/professional mentor often means encouraging your mentees to do things they might not consider doing on their own. Audrey said that her mentor pushed her to present at a conference:

> My first mentor liked a program that I did, and said, "You should really present on this." And I said, "Well I've never done that before." And she said, "Oh well, I'm going to sign you up for this conference then, and we'll go together. I'll be there, and I'll watch, and I'll cheer you on, and you'll present this program." So, I did, and it was lovely, and then I had that checked off and under my belt, boom, I've presented at a conference.

When Fred moved to a public library, he was nervous about his lack of public speaking experience, which was a requirement of the new job. His boss mentored him through the learning curve.

my boss at the time used to go out and she would make presentations ... and she started inviting me to come along, and then we would divide it up. She would do three quarters, and I would do one quarter kind of thing.

Kat spoke about the impact of mentorship from a senior manager during the early stages of Kat's career:

She would encourage me to take – whenever a library branch manager might have to take an extended leave, go be that temporary library manager, build up your experience, and that was what let me be able to become the [city]-wide coordinator for young adult services. I was the manager of young adult services for the whole [city] within five years of starting as a permanent librarian in the state system.

Kat was ready and able to move up the career ladder thanks to the experience that her mentor pushed her to get.

Institutional mentor

An institutional mentor can be an important connection, especially in the early days of a new job. When a new librarian starts at the authors' university, they are assigned this type of mentor, typically another librarian in their department. The institutional mentor helps them orient to the department, library, and broader university. This ranges from helping make sense of the bureaucracy, to understanding who does what, to deciphering the local jargon and long list of acronyms. An assigned institutional mentor gives the new librarian someone they can feel free to ask questions of, without feeling they are being a bother. This isn't a substitute for an institutional orientation process, but rather a supplement.

If being assigned an institutional mentor isn't part of your onboarding process, you may want to bring up the concept to your supervisor and ask if they could suggest someone. If that's not comfortable, you may prefer to approach someone who has seemed open and helpful already. They don't have to be a librarian; consider experienced staff or non-MLIS administrators, too. The person should work at your library but not be part of your reporting chain. That way, you can be comfortable asking "simple" questions without fearing a negative performance appraisal.

Conference mentor

This is an easy, low-stakes way to get your feet wet with mentorship. Some conferences offer opportunities to get connected to a conference mentor, sometimes called conference friend or buddy. This opportunity may come through email lists or message boards, or the conference may offer it as an opt-in during the registration process. The conference mentor can help you make your conference experience better: from figuring out how to navigate the exhibits hall to explaining committee work to untangling a packed schedule to which social events to attend. The informal nature of this mentorship lends itself to frequent small encounters, like meeting over coffee or attending a vendor reception together. Depending on how well you connect, you two might stay in touch and the relationship could evolve into a broader mentorship. The connection may simply mean that you now have a friendly acquaintance to meet up with at next year's conference. If there's no connection, then it's just a case of nothing ventured, nothing gained.

Life coach or fan

Though this may not be what you think of when you hear the word "mentor," it is important to have someone in your life who voices their full-throated support and will talk things through when you need to. This person doesn't necessarily need to be in the library field, much less in your library; they just need to care about you and your success and be willing and able to communicate with you. You can unabashedly tell them about your career highs without feeling like you're bragging; you can discuss new opportunities knowing that they want the best for you; they listen to your concerns without being judgmental. Jenn turned to her partner:

> having that partner in my life was able to help me, he's just a good listener, really. So, he was able to help me kind of work through, I needed a sounding board in some cases, and it was only ever five minutes after work kind of thing and then move on, switch gears, do something else because you can't do that. But having a good friend or having a good person or group of people in your life who can help you and at least hear you out for a few minutes and then help you work through something just to think out loud, because I like to think out loud sometimes.

You may well have someone in your life like this already – you just might not think of them as a mentor. If you're not sure who might fill this role in your life, take a moment to think about those closest to you. Who do you tell first when you receive good news? Who can cheer you up when you've had a bad day? This person may not understand the finer points of your job, but they should be supportive of your success and struggles alike.

Community mentor

If you've relocated for your new position, you may find yourself in an unfamiliar town with no prior contacts. In this scenario, look for a community mentor. This is the person who can tell you the best place to get pizza, fun local events and attractions, and offer tips about transportation and local government. You may even want more than one community mentor.

For example, one person may be a good source for doctors and home repair professionals, while another has afterschool ideas for your kids. This is an informal kind of mentorship, and it's likely your community mentor(s) will not even know that you consider them such. This is one of the easier mentors to find, as most people enjoy being asked their opinions. They may even introduce you to future friends.

Beyond personal needs and interests, there are also professional reasons to learn the community. You need to learn about the populations that your library serves and the area it is situated in. Jodie stressed the importance of this: "If you're moving into a community that you don't know, you need to get the know the community quickly. That's a really, really big thing." Learning about the community can help you understand what to expect from your patrons, and help you learn where they're coming from.

Peer mentors and support groups

Another great way to find unexpected mentorship is to join a support group. Your institution may already have a formal group for new employees that you can join. If not, perhaps you could create an informal group of peers at a new employee orientation, training, or similar. A few fellow newbies getting coffee and talking once a month or so is a great resource as you all get acclimated to the institution and share new insights. This group is likely to comprise people from all around your new organization, not just the library, and will give you a different perspective and bigger view of your new job.

A peer mentor is often the colleague down the hall or the one you share an office with. Lisa's mentor helped her transition from being an academic librarian to becoming an assistant professor of library science:

> I think this goes to the importance of ... mentors. And I do have one. The person who I work with who I took over from sabbatical ... we share an office right now and we work really closely together. ... I think that's really important to have that mentor to have someone who can tell you what the real deal is and tell you who the people are that you need to talk to. I think that's really important for new people like new librarians coming into the field or people who are shifting maybe context or sectors I guess, but also experienced people ... I think it's still really important to have that person who you know you can count on and ask questions and not feel silly.

Sometimes peer mentors are at other libraries, often nearby. They have jobs similar to yours and can share ideas and relatable experiences. When Jodie started as CEO of a library in Canada, she said that "all of the other CEOs [in the county] were very welcoming, and I could ask them questions. So, having that mentorship helped a lot. And if I didn't have that, I would have really, really struggled."

Kady has found her officemates to be a very helpful support, especially as she transitioned in from another size and type of library.

> There are librarians working in my office who have been – I mean one's about to retire in a couple weeks – been working specifically in this system for 30 years. And just their knowledge; I check in with them a lot about ... somebody asked for this book and, it's sort of borderline, and just talking through that kind of stuff, and then broader issues. It's been really useful. There have been a lot of people ... that have really helped. ... it hasn't been a traditional mentor-mentee relationship. It's like peer mentors and we help each other through those questions and career path issues and everything else.

You may find, too, that you can learn from someone in your library that you don't necessarily like. They aren't someone you want to emulate completely. For example, you may not appreciate the way a colleague organizes her work, but she is incredibly active in professional organizations and could give you wonderful tips on how to get involved. It's perfectly natural to have a wide variety of people you consider "mentors" for different aspects of your job.

Self-mentorship (or, finding support when you're on your own)

Sometimes librarianship can be a lonely path. You may find yourself the only librarian of your type at your new library or perhaps you're now a solo librarian or working remotely. Even in a building full of people, you may not click with anyone right away. This can be freeing, but also has challenges. How do you learn from your colleagues when they're not there? Self-mentorship is a way for you to push yourself to grow professionally on your own. Set aside time on a regular basis to reflect on your career, develop over-arching goals, identify your skill gaps, and then work to improve them. If you're having trouble making goals for yourself or deciding on a skill to learn, look over Chapter 2 Exploring New Opportunities for some ideas on career reinvention. Look for a variety of options to avoid isolation, such as conferences, online webinars, email lists, social media platforms for librarians, and support/peer groups of other professionals in similar circumstances.

Jodie spoke to us about the importance of seeking connection outside the library:

> When you're the only person, the only children's librarian or the only CEO or the only school librarian in the building you sometimes feel like you're alone. It's like, OK, well, I need this for my puppet program. Well, nobody else understand why you're doing puppets. So, being able to get online, like "OK, I'm doing this puppet program, what do you think?" "Oh yeah, that's a great idea!" So, having the outside world connections are very, very important.

Several of our interviewees mentioned using social media as a mentorship and support mechanism. Audrey said that "If I were getting out of library school today, I would definitely take advantage of the support available and advice available on social media." Though Jinnie also had a great mentor, she told us "I have a really good support network on social media, Twitter and Facebook." This doesn't require travel and is ongoing throughout the year.

Other kinds of learning from colleagues and associates

You may not be inclined toward a formal mentor. Deb said,

> Formal mentors, no. I'm kind of an individualist; I don't like having that kind of relationship. But looking back, there are certainly people who influenced me greatly, and who I would think about when I was making decisions, what they would do.

Marian had a similar take:

> I have always watched what other people were doing and learned from other people ... others that I would just read everything they wrote. It wasn't like a mentorship where they knew it was going on. But I would pick out people in the profession and colleagues I had that I thought were doing a great job, and I would just learn from them in that way. I pay a lot of attention to what people do.

Deb and Marian's manner of utilizing the example of others fits with Kathy's concept of the kind of mentoring she's provided: "Have I served as a mentor?" Kathy said. "I don't know. I think I've served as an example."

Yolanda told us about some lessons she took away from a leadership seminar:

> everybody in some way or shape or form is going to be a mentor to you. Even the custodians are your mentors – and they can give you advice that others wouldn't ever be able to give you. So never count anyone out, never look down on anybody because everybody is helpful and teaching you something about what you do. ... You might hate someone or not really like someone that you work with, but they can still teach you lessons, like they still have good things to offer, and you have to look at that and try not to be consumed with your feelings about that person.

Finding mentors

We've discussed numerous ways to find mentors in the sections above. We'll summarize them here, so the ideas are easy to find:

- Find each other at work.
- Sign up for mentorship programs through conferences.
- Many library associations have mentorship programs, matching people according to goals or interests. Pam told us about such a program started by her library association: "they have a practice where they set mentors up in different organizations. Somebody who's just starting in management, for example, they'll set them up with an experienced manager in a completely different institution somewhere else, and they just navigate that interaction outside the workplace."
- Networking. Ask colleagues or friends in the profession if they can recommend someone qualified to talk to you about your desired field. An introduction via a mutual acquaintance may be more likely to gain a response than a cold call or email.
- Professional email lists and other kinds of social media: pay attention to whose posts are most useful to you and consider contacting them. We've seen someone request a mentor via the social media platform of a national library association with apparent success.
- See if the alumni association of your library school offers any mentoring opportunities.
- Keep your eyes open when you attend training or take further coursework. Jodie found a group of peer-mentors over the course of a two-year leadership program.
- When you've identified someone who you think would be a great fit as a mentor for you, you can either formally ask them or see if it happens organically. If you are nervous about asking, keep in mind that this question is extremely flattering. Think about how you feel when someone says that they admire a skillset of yours, or specialized knowledge that you have. While a simple, "Would you be willing to mentor me?" may be adequate, and may well meet with success, your potential mentor will likely have follow-up questions. Instead, consider asking something more specific, like "I think your career has been really interesting, particularly how you were able to transition between departments and into leadership. Would you be open to becoming my mentor? I'm thinking we could get coffee (or talk online, etc.) once a month or so and chat." This highlights why you want this person to be your mentor and indicates the approximate time commitment you're imagining. If you're still uncomfortable, consider Maureen's advice: "Reach out and if you can, get a mentor that is at the type of library you want to be at, or with the organization you would like to join. Reach out; network. Even if it's not a formal mentorship, because a lot of us will share our knowledge and we want to help others succeed. I have yet to meet a librarian that doesn't feel that way." Sharing knowledge is at the heart of librarianship.

Becoming a mentor

When do you know enough to become someone else's mentor? There isn't a set goal line, or a day you'll wake up magically feeling like you've ascended into the next plane. Instead, consider where you are in your knowledge and experience. Even someone just a few years into a library job may be fully capable of mentoring someone who is brand new to the workforce. We all have things we wish someone had told us at the beginning of our careers. Just because you have mentors for your career doesn't mean you can't effectively mentor someone else at the same time. The world is not split into people who are "mentors" and people who are "mentees." Everyone can be both.

Many of our interviewees spoke about mentoring other librarians, especially those who are at the beginning of their careers. Andy told us, "I do work as a mentor with some younger staff members (again, nobody I directly manage) and find it massively rewarding."

Maureen said,

> I was hoping to be a mentor to others because I think that is a huge benefit to someone starting out, is having that someone who has been through some of these road blocks that you're going to encounter and you don't know which way to turn to or what do I do. I would have liked to have that at the beginning.

Fred also has served as a mentor:

> I've also mentored people over the years, too. When I was at the [library], two clerical people that I mentored went on to get their MLS ... Here again I've tried to give some guidance to people particularly through volunteer associations, being active particularly in the [state] library association, giving advice to new librarians.

If you would like to mentor new librarians, a good place to start is where those new librarians are minted. Contact your library school (or the one most convenient to you) and see if they run a mentorship matching program. If not, consider volunteering to start one. For other options for becoming a mentor, see the section above about finding a mentor. You want to be where the potential mentees are looking.

Qualities of a mentor

A mentor should be willing to listen, make themselves available, and suggest paths to solve problems. When talking about what makes a good mentor, Ronit spoke about a mentor of hers who "was always available for answering questions. She was really great at connecting me with people in the library community, and she somehow just knew a lot about different areas." Look for these qualities in anyone you approach for mentorship and be sure to reflect them with anyone you are mentoring.

Mentors should be on the lookout for signs of burnout or impostor syndrome in their mentees, particularly if the mentee is undergoing a big job transition. In their article "Addressing Psychosocial Factors with Library Mentoring," Farrell et al. note that burnout can be intensified in librarians experiencing impostor syndrome or racial microaggressions (2017). They advocate for mentors to first be aware of burnout, impostor syndrome, and microaggressions so that they can then respond appropriately if their mentees bring up these issues or experiences. As a mentor, it's your responsibility to take your mentee's concerns and experiences seriously without being dismissive.

Age doesn't matter

The traditional concept of a mentor is usually someone older than the mentee. But older isn't a requirement. Librarianship is often a second career, so an older librarian may well have less experience than a younger one. Or the younger mentor may simply have more experience in the desired sector of the field or with a particular situation. Jinnie was matched with a mentor much younger than her and greatly enjoyed the experience.

> I have a really wonderful mentor who has stayed with me. We got placed together when I was in the University ... program, but she has continued to be my mentor even though she is 30 years my junior. A phenomenal mentor, she's really wonderful. She's been really wonderfully supportive.

Short-term or long-term

Expect to have multiple mentors and/or mentees over your career. People's needs and availability change. Like friendships, mentoring relationships are sometimes specific to a certain set of circumstances and they fade when those circumstances change. Other relationships persist for the long run. While long-term relationships are wonderful, that doesn't diminish the value of what you can learn from and give to a briefer mentorship.

It's a two-way street

The best mentoring relationships are very much a two-way street. Our interviewee Kady worked with Tina when they were both at a previous institution. Kady considered Tina to be a mentor, but Tina thinks that she herself also benefitted tremendously from their connection and learned a lot from Kady. This was an informal mentorship that developed organically as they tackled several large projects together. In some cases, the work that needed to be done was new to both and they figured it out together, with one or the other taking the lead as they were able to. This speaks to another reality of

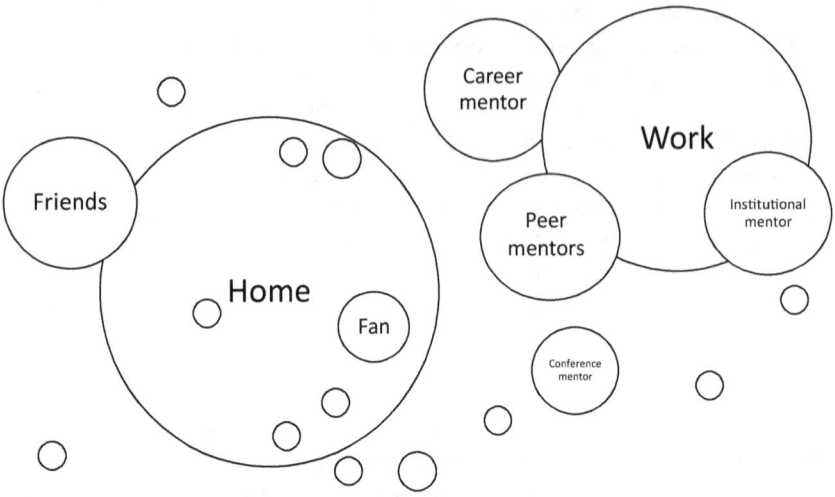

Figure 4.1 Mentorship bubble chart.

the mentor relationship: the mentor doesn't always have the answers. Some problems and circumstances require a team approach. Expect to slide back and forth between being a teacher and a learner. Be open to admitting that you don't know something, regardless of your years of experience. Take the opportunity to learn together.

Support system summary

Making a big change can be overwhelming, but you likely already have a support system. Take stock of where you are, and look for types of mentors who can fill in the gaps. Figure 4.1 illustrates the overlapping nature of these various types of mentorship.

Questions for self-reflection and planning

1. What is your ultimate career goal? Who has this job that you could connect with?
2. Who is your fan? Are you a fan for someone else?
3. What do you wish you had known before you started your first library job?
4. What do you see new librarians do that you would advise against?
5. What are three areas or topics of librarianship in which you could mentor another librarian?
6. List three colleagues, past or present, that impress you. What are their strengths? What do you want to learn from them?

7. What opportunities do you have to connect with a mentor or mentee? Consider the list under "Finding a Mentor" and select two or three options to investigate.
8. Start a list of questions you would like to ask a mentor. Is there someone (or a specific social media platform or email list) whom you could ask any of these questions today? Consider if you already have access to mentors who can address some of your questions.

References

Farrell, B., Alabi, J., Whaley, P., & Jenda, C. (2017). Addressing Psychosocial Factors with Library Mentoring. *Portal: Libraries and the Academy*, 17(1), 51–69. https://doi.org/10.1353/pla.2017.0004

James, J. M., Rayner, A., & Bruno, J. (2015). Are You My Mentor? New Perspectives and Research on Informal Mentorship. *Journal of Academic Librarianship*, 41(5), 532–539. https://doi.org/10.1016/j.acalib.2015.07.009

5 Being the new person

When you're the new librarian at the library, there's a lot to learn, much more than the human resources onboarding tells you. This chapter helps the new employee adjust successfully. The authors provide ideas for learning each part of your new environment: the library; departments; the online tools and software; the municipality, campus, or institution beyond the library; and the consortia. Suggestions are given for using committees, events, email lists, new employee groups, and more to enhance orientation. The new human environment is important, too: what are your new supervisor's goals? What most concerns your staff? Get to know your new colleagues and their priorities. Tips are given for learning your job and adjusting to differences from the old way. Deal with new job brain fog. If you've moved, get acquainted to your new geographic area. Learn the community around the library. The chapter gives advice from interviewees who have experience in being the new person, including accepting the need to ask lots of questions and to identify important external orientation factors such as finding the coffeeshop on the way to work. The chapter concludes with questions for reflection.

Changing your assumptions and expectations

One of the more disorienting aspects of moving to a new type of library is not knowing some foundational information. What is important varies from place to place. For example, tracking and maintaining perpetual access to online scholarly journals is critical to a research university library, but probably isn't on the radar for public libraries and some smaller academics. Having enough copies of the latest bestsellers, in multiple formats, is critical in a public library, while an academic might just want a few popular titles in a browsing collection and may try to avoid duplication altogether. A willingness to help out anywhere and anytime you're needed is important in small libraries, but similar behavior could be seen as intrusive in larger ones.

While you are new, it's important to recognize that bedrock assumptions in your old library may not hold in the new one. Remembering to question your own assumptions and to ask for clarification is key. Being new is a gift! You have a window where your colleagues will not expect you to know how to do things and will be happy to offer their expertise. Use this window to gather and document as much as possible, and then return to your notes whenever needed as you settle into your job and take on new tasks.

What resources are available to you?

Most libraries have an onboarding process to help new hires adjust and get up to speed. This can be a series of trainings, one-on-one meetings with various department heads, a set time where you "shadow" someone and watch how they do their job, or a large packet of documents that you're meant to read through on your own. Ideally, the onboarding process should include a combination of all of the above. Of course, not every library will have an airtight process, and even the best training will still leave knowledge gaps. Regardless of your library's training package, you will need to supplement with self-directed research.

First, take time to find and document all the various resources that are available to you. Are you now part of a campus or municipality? Check with your new human resources department and see what trainings are available. Many municipalities and universities offer a wide range of scheduled seminars covering a host of topics from managing money to navigating the process of supervising others. You may have access to a subscription service like LinkedIn Learning that teaches a wide variety of technical skills. If you do not wish to commit to attending anything right off the bat, just note what types of trainings are offered and come back to them when you feel you are ready. At a very large institution, you may be linked from the HR webpage to many other departments that offer classes or trainings, such as technology courses from IT or safety classes from the police. Take note of any that appeal to you; in addition to learning new skills, these represent an opportunity to meet people across the institution or municipality.

Next, consider resources outside of your institution. Are you part of a consortium? How about a multi-type library organization? Is there a government department related to libraries for your state or province? Many of these types of organizations offer a variety of library-related trainings. In Florida, the State Library maintains a continuing education portal for in-state library employees, for example. Add these different training sites to your list, along with what information you'll need to log into any portals. Many consortia require you to have permissions to log into their trainings, and you may need to request this from your supervisor or HR. Some libraries belong to a fee-based consortia organization such as Amigos or Lyrasis in the United States; they are independent organizations that provide a variety of services to the libraries at a cost. Training may be available through them at a reduced fee if your library already uses one of their other services, such as consortia purchasing.

Then, consider your professional affiliations. What organizations are you a member of? Even if you've been a member for years, go to their websites and review their resources. Now that you're in a new environment, you can consider the training materials from a new perspective and may discover some that suddenly seem appealing. If you are moving from a small library to a large one, you may find detailed guides that were too involved for your work previously that get into the level of specialty you need for your new position. Conversely, if you're moving to a smaller library, you may want to broaden your search and look at resources from professional organizations for each aspect of your job. You can go deep into resources in the areas you now specialize in, and skim in areas you're newly taking on. You're likely also in the market for new professional organizations to join, whether due to being in a new type of library, new geographic location, working with new resources or programs that are associated with different organizations or conferences, or a combination of these factors. Chapter 7 discusses ways to find these new potential affiliations.

This information resource audit will be a helpful reference throughout the first few months on the job. Even if you aren't relocating geographically and had many of these same resources available at your previous position, a resource audit like this can be really helpful. At your previous job, you probably already knew how to do what was expected of you and were confident in your skills to accomplish those tasks. You may have even been too bogged down in the day-to-day work to consider what other skills you would like to learn. It can be hard to let yourself think about acquiring new abilities when you're overworked or don't see an immediate practical use for them. A new job is a new opportunity to consider what skills you want or need to learn.

Finally, heed Marian's advice for getting oriented:

> I ask a lot of questions. A lot of questions. And I am not at all embarrassed to say, "I don't know" and I am not embarrassed to ask the same person the same question multiple times over the course of say 3 or 4 months. If I have to do a task that's difficult or that it's not clear what the process is – I will keep asking. So I spent a lot of time asking questions. I spent a lot of time getting to know people. When I came here ... I made the assumption that the people who were already here knew what was going on and they were going to be my experts. And they were. They had the history of the place, they knew what had happened before with the previous director, they knew what issues were going on with the public, where there was happiness about what we did, and discontent with what we did, they knew what we had been ordering ... So I talked to them, extensively talked to them. I do a lot of reading; I do a lot of watching. I try not to make big changes quickly. I just take my time trying to just understand what's going on and soaking up as much information as I can. But I ask a lot of questions.

What is the librarians' focus?

You should have a bit of an idea about the focus of your job from the position description and interview, though occasionally position descriptions are written by HR and may be of limited help in describing your actual work. Talk with the other librarians and consider what their focus is. Do they talk a lot about upcoming conference presentations they're giving or papers they're submitting? Are they discussing a particularly interesting reference question that just came in? When they are at their busiest, are they still always available to meet with students working on assignments? Get a sense of their priorities.

At some libraries, customer service will be a big issue and the main focus. These types of libraries want a personal touch, to see that everyone who wants to talk with someone connects with a person who can help them. Other libraries may not have the staff to do a such a high-touch customer-oriented plan and will focus instead on figuring out ways to help the patrons help themselves, pushing out high-quality online tutorials or seminars that teach many users at once. It's important to know what kind of situation you're walking into – is this a library that is trying to increase usage, or a library that is trying to meet overwhelming demand?

Knowing her primary clientele was central to Lisa's efforts to get oriented in a new environment: at the academic library, her primary clientele was the people she helped at the reference desk. As a professor, it's her students. "That to me has always grounded me and has helped me know or figure out what's going on. As long as you're good with your primary clientele, everything else will work itself out. You'll figure it out."

Software and online tools

Of course, it's not just your physical environment that changes when you begin a new job, your online environment can be uprooted as well. Whether it's working in a new Integrated Library System (ILS) or discovering a new portfolio of software available to you, adapting to your new digital space can take some time.

Check to see whether your IT department lists various software programs that you can download and install. At many libraries, employees will have to request that IT install programs, rather than handling it on their own. It's helpful to know all the programs that you need so that you only have to go through this process once. This is also an opportunity to ask about free software that you'd like to use that you don't see listed anywhere. Some IT departments will want to vet your request before granting you permission to install it, so you'll want to give yourself plenty of time for the process.

There may also be software or web tools that have limited seats, which means that you'll have to request access rather than have access automatically.

Hopefully, these things are spelled out on your IT department's web page. If not, ask or run some questions past your institutional mentor (see Chapter 4).

Something to consider at this stage is how your library organizes their files. Many libraries, particularly large institutions, will have a robust shared drive or shared repository. What information are you expected to save in a place where others can easily access it? If you are on a library committee, does that committee have an online space? Moving from a library that doesn't have a shared drive to one that does (or vice versa) can take some getting used to. When you go to your first committee meeting, or meet with a new department head, ask if they have a shared folder and if you should have access to it.

In addition to shared folders, many libraries have a space where they maintain data from local, national, international, or association-run surveys or reports. If you have access to this information, you can learn about the institution from a larger perspective and it may put some priorities in perspective. Poking around this shared space (assuming you're permitted) is also a great way to get a handle on what other projects people have been working on, or how statistics have changed over the years.

Lastly, be prepared to need a tutorial on how to use the phones at your new library. Calling inside or outside the institution may require different codes or permissions. Nothing makes you feel like a newbie like having to ask how to make or receive a phone call.

Figuring out your library's priorities

We've touched on this a bit with finding the librarians' focus, but the library as a whole has many written and unwritten priorities that you'll need to understand. The written priorities will be the easiest to track down, as they are likely published in the library's annual report or strategic plan. If your library doesn't have such a report, it may have a mission and vision statement. It's likely that your library must report on a number of goals up through the bureaucracy. If these aren't posted publicly, you could ask your supervisor or a knowledgeable colleague.

The written, official goals or priorities can be helpful, but sometimes you may feel they are full of jargon, or ultimately meaningless for your work. You'll want to try to learn the unofficial, or unwritten priorities as well. However, these can be trickier to find. One way to get started is to make a connection with a senior colleague. If you have meetings scheduled with department heads and administrators as a part of your onboarding process, this is a great way to get a bead on unwritten goals. Ask for clarification about stated library priorities and how those priorities tie into their departments. Another option is to ask about primary goals for their area in the coming year. If this sounds too formal for you, simply ask them what library projects they are excited about.

You can also learn a lot about your library's priorities through observation. Many user-experience exercises involve choosing a task that a patron might want to accomplish and then tracing every step they must take to complete it. For example, pay attention to the barriers a patron faces when trying to use online resources and consider why those barriers exist. If a library requires patrons to log in to use databases, even when physically in the library, there may be cost-based, technical, or legal reasons behind that. Making these sorts of observations can lead to many interesting conversations with colleagues that will help you understand what's going on around you. Depending on your area, this exercise might be done with librarians or staff tasks, too, and could help you get a handle on what your direct reports deal with day in and day out.

Don't make changes right away

You might start seeing things that you want to change or fix right away. Decisions might not make sense or processes could seem inefficient. Make note of these, but it's strongly suggested to not make big changes right away. This advice was echoed by many of our interviewees, such as Maureen: "I would recommend people to give themselves time and not jump and just assume they know what needs are there. Really look at it."

Wait, watch, and ask questions about why things are done. Learn the "whys" before making changes. What made sense in your previous institution could be a bad idea in the new place. Trust that there are complexities that aren't obvious at first. In addition, your new colleagues will need a little time to get used to you (and vice versa). Asking questions – and listening closely – in order to learn and understand will likely be welcome; pointing out everything that seems wrong is usually off-putting.

Fighting the new job brain fog

When Sara began her new job, she was surprised at how mentally exhausted she was every evening. It seemed like everything was moving so quickly, her first six months flew by in a whirlwind. She was still excited to absorb a ton of new information and tackle so many new tasks, but she also felt drained and found her memory failing her. She mentioned this is in passing to Tina, her institutional mentor (see Chapter 4), who was relatively new herself, and Tina replied that she had felt the same way for about the first year. Tina adopted the phrase "new job brain fog" to explain the memory lapses and exhaustion that they had both been feeling.

Another symptom of "new job brain fog" is forgetting how to do things you've done many times before. You may have taken a few weeks off between jobs to relocate or take a vacation. When you begin your new job, your mind is taking in so many things at once, you may forget how to use a particular database or a certain piece of software. Cut yourself some slack, and don't be afraid to ask for help from colleagues. Take some time to reacquaint yourself to your tools and systems, particularly if you took time off between jobs.

Should you experience "new job brain fog," it's important to know that this is temporary! You will begin to return to your normal state. In the meantime, here are some easy ways to combat it and take care of yourself.

Write everything down. Always keep a notebook and pen (or digital equivalent) with you during your first few months on the job and take notes. Even when you are in a meeting with a designated note-taker, write down your own notes. There will be so many things that people gloss over in these meetings, you need to note items to investigate further, such as acronyms you don't understand and unfamiliar projects to ask about. It's also important to write things down even if you feel lost in the meeting. Whether you take notes by hand or digitally is up to personal preference, but it is helpful to type up your handwritten notes or otherwise digitize them later so that you can easily search them. Those notes may not be meaningful at the time, but you will eventually be able to make sense of them. Periodically review your notes and you'll be surprised as you start to connect the dots.

During this period of transition, it's important to practice self-care. When you are fighting the "new job brain fog," you may be inclined to keep your head down and power through. You want to work longer hours because you're trying to figure things out and get yourself on track. However, it is absolutely vital that you allow yourself to take breaks. Just getting up from your desk every couple of hours and walking around is a great way to mentally reset and refresh yourself. If you can go outside to walk, do that. Walking around the library can be helpful as well, and a great excuse to orient yourself to your new surroundings. At home, you might need more sleep than usual and might not have the mental or physical energy for some of your usual non-work pastimes. Cut yourself slack in these areas too. Your body and brain will adapt as you adjust.

Yolanda echoes the call to cut yourself some slack:

> what could I do myself to make all the transitions work is – and here's the weird thing – to be a little bit more gentle with myself and realize that I am new and there's no way I can know everything the first day. And just be okay with the fact that you maybe want to hit the ground running, but you're only going to be able to hit the ground skipping. And that's on me. So, that's the thing I have to do. I have to be like, you know what, it's okay if I'm not running this first semester because I can't, because how could I? How could I know everything that I need to know to be able to run?

Learning your job

There is a learning curve for everyone starting a new job, even for those with a lot of experience. Many processes will be similar, but every library has their workflows. For example, in acquisitions, books arrive, get processed, paid for, and moved along to be cataloged. This basic process happens at nearly every library. But within that basic workflow, there are many opportunities for divergence: will the books arrive already physically processed? Will bibliographic records come with the book orders? Do they need to be loaded into the system or otherwise enabled? How many different vendors supply books to your library, and are there different workflows for each? What system do you have to keep track of orders? Your new library might have vendors doing much more or much less than you're used to. The number of people and departments involved can vary greatly between sizes and types, too. Processes that were very familiar to you from your prior library can be quite different at the new place.

When trying to learn her job at a new library, Audrey asks,

> What are your expectations for the person in this job, what do you expect to see for benchmarks for doing this job appropriately or well, and how do I meet them now that I'm here? What steps do I need to take to get into that groove? That's sort of the goal for your first few months, is figuring out what do they want from you, and how are you going to give it to them and add value to the organization. I guess that's more intellectual level rather than just "where's the bathroom?" But honestly, if you don't have both of them then it's not going to work so well.

These differences can be quite disconcerting until you adapt. Tina performed or directly oversaw every step of monographic acquisitions and cataloging at her small academic library. After moving to the very large university, she had an odd sense of things being out of control when she saw that these steps were spread out across two departments and at least a dozen people. These feelings arose despite Tina's earlier experience in large public library systems. Her mind knew the process would involve lots of people at a larger library, but the feeling that it was unmanageable still came. Accept that you may have feelings and emotions that don't make objective sense. We absorb and learn in a variety of ways.

To get yourself oriented to how your library works, borrow some techniques from the user experience realm. First, write down any parts of your job that interact with the user, like working on the reference desk or providing library instruction. Then, choose one to start with, and write down every single step a patron would take to get to the point where you're interacting with them. By doing this, you'll get a clearer picture of the reality of the library. You can also adapt this to back office processes and functions if you need to figure out the staff workings. Instead of tracing a user, trace the path an invoice takes, or a book. Think of a task that happens in your library and follow its path from person to person. This will help you understand who is truly involved in each step.

But, above all, be patient with yourself and give yourself time to learn the full extent of your job. Jodie said that she really needed a full year before she understood everything.

> My first six months, I did my evaluation and I rated myself very high, like "I know what I'm doing, I'm doing great." And then the one year hit, and I went, oh my goodness, you were so naïve, you did not know what you were doing.

Kady felt similarly, saying,

> A one year cycle goes with this job, a budget cycle or a school year ... So the second year is where I think you're really fine tuning and testing, and still learning ... Two years is really what it takes to settle in and be like, "ok, I've got a handle on this."

Learning your library and institution

Libraries can be very complex organisms. Changing library sizes or types brings you into contact with a much different animal. Though many different types of libraries have analogous departments, it's very likely that you will see a different configuration in your new library structure.

How is the library organized?

A great tool for a new librarian is an organizational chart of your new library. This may change a bit each year as people retire, leave, or are hired. Go through the various departments on the chart and note any that are new to you or seem a little vaguely named. Do a little research into what they do. Try researching the librarians working in those departments to see what conference presentations they've given, or what papers they've written. See if there is a professional organization for those types of librarians. Most professional organizations have a pretty succinct summary of the topic on their webpage. You may not be working with those departments regularly but try to get a handle on what they do, in case you want to collaborate in the future.

What has the library accomplished?

You'll also want to look through your library's previous annual reports. Many libraries have these published in an institutional repository or posted on their website. Reports from the past five years should be sufficient to see what projects were recently completed, what goals have been met, and what the trends are. Don't feel compelled to memorize or look at every bit of data. Most people aren't expected to know the entire history of the library (at least not right away) and besides, they hired you for a fresh point of view.

These reports can help you in multiple ways. You'll likely be expected to contribute to at least some of these reports in the future, so you'll have a sense of what they entail. Note the major changes or accomplishments from each year, and who was involved. See how the budget has fluctuated from year to year, how usage patterns are evolving, and what types of outreach and programming is happening. Knowing what others have been working on can be a great help as you start to get involved in committees and projects. When you get a great idea, you'll be able to make connections to past projects or bring in other librarians with appropriate expertise.

What reports are available?

Every library will have its own configuration for reports and statistics. Even if you are familiar with the ILS or other systems that your new library uses, you may find that the local implementation is unfamiliar. For example, Sara moved between two Florida libraries within the same consortium and same ILS. However, the new library had a different implementation of the ILS, and there was an entirely separate reports module. Her favorite report from her first library couldn't be accessed at her new library due to those implementation decisions. It was an unexpected learning curve to figure out a way around this deficiency.

Depending on your job needs, spend the time needed to learn what reporting software is available and how to run reports or if they are run automatically. In the latter case, find out how you get access to those reports. Many libraries have been gathering statistics in the same manner for quite some time, and as a new librarian you have a great opportunity to ask questions about why the library gathers the information and what is done with it.

Who are you working with?

A wonderful thing about starting a new job is meeting your new colleagues. There are so many different paths into librarianship, and so many twists and turns that library careers can take, your new colleagues probably have a wide range of backgrounds and expertise. Advice on connecting with people varies depending on personality type. If you are outgoing and find it very easy to talk to people, you may see this section as simple common sense. But those of us with anxiety in some social situations can use a primer. Introverts should plan quiet time, to the degree possible, between various interactions with new people. Know your limits and space out the meetings, lunches, etc. as appropriate to your own needs.

Start with the people you'll be working with most closely. Hopefully, someone will introduce you around but if not, a friendly smile and greeting will do the job. If there's a staff directory online (especially if it has photos), that's a big help in remembering names and faces.

You may find yourself moving into a department where you are the only new person and everyone else has been there for decades. There are a lot of positives to such a situation, such as a wealth of experience and institutional knowledge you can draw on. There are some downsides, too. Many librarians who have been in one place for a long time have a tendency not to document things at the same rate as librarians who have moved around. A librarian who moved within five years will be much more aware of what needs to be written down for other people than someone who has been at the same job for a while. They may remember all of the details in their head, or they may rely on their extensive email archive. Either way, if it isn't documented, you'll need to ask questions.

Pam transitioned from being a teaching faculty to becoming a librarian in an academic library. Many things were new to her and she was able to share the learning experience with a colleague who had also transitioned from being a teaching faculty.

> I was very lucky that there was a – I had another colleague who was also a faculty librarian and changed to academic librarian and she was very knowledgeable. And we just shared a lot of information. I did a lot of research to make sure I understood those topics well and what I found out, I shared with her. It was a really great collegial relationship.

Your new boss or supervisor is an important component of this new group of colleagues. Marian offers insight into communicating with them effectively:

> when I'm dealing with my supervisors and bosses, I try to talk in terms of what I know their goals are, what is it they want to achieve, what is it they want this library to achieve, and I try to speak to them in that language so that we have a common understanding of what I ought to be doing.

This is obviously predicated on your knowing what your boss or supervisor's goals are; there's a good topic for an early, and perhaps ongoing, conversation with them.

Librarians and administration are, of course, not the only people worth talking to. Many of our interviewees talked about how they gained the most insight at their new position by talking to their staff, particularly if they were moving into a supervisory role. Anna said that,

> I do a lot of talking to junior and senior staff, because I think often senior staff doesn't have the level of detail that junior staff do. Or staff who spend more time on the desk are often more aware of issues that come up over and over again, whereas a manager might only deal with it once a month. It doesn't feel quite the same way.

Connecting to other parts of the organization outside the library

The municipality, campus, or institution beyond the library is also worth your attention. Getting a sense of the broader realm will help you understand the place of the library and prevent tunnel vision. You can raise your own profile and be a positive face for the library. Being new, you may be able to connect with people or departments who have shied away from working with the library in the past for reasons best forgotten and associated with people long gone.

Anna agreed with this sentiment and gave us an example from her experience:

> Being able to seek ways of making connections that people who have always worked there might not see, that can be quite a useful skill. If you get into a conversation that other people have wanted to get into and not been able to, that's certainly something I've managed to do. Moving between roles, it's made me more successful. When I joined the city, I got on really well with IT, because that's what I'd done in my previous role. And the library had always struggled to understand IT, and IT had always struggled with the library. And because of that, when I joined the city, that ability to kind of think of things a different way, because I was used to dealing with them in a different way, helped a lot to resolve a lot of long-term IT issues, which in turn kind of promoted my stock a bit, I suppose, and encouraged people to think favorably of me.

Making contacts outside the library can help you manage your transition on social and personal fronts. When people start to recognize you, or remember your name, you start to feel a sense of belonging. Introduce yourself to unfamiliar faces when you're out and about; being new is a great excuse to meet people.

How do you make these connections? Keep an open mind when opportunities arise. There will likely be a call for people to serve on the parking task force, an announcement of a support group for junior faculty, or an opportunity to represent the library at a local civic group. You may be asked – or told – to serve on a committee. Say yes to at least one of these opportunities. If you are somewhere very small and there aren't regular calls for committee members or new groups forming, ask your supervisor for suggestions. Most supervisors will like that you want to get more involved in the organization – it shows passion and dedication for your job.

Other possibilities include a consortium or multi-type library organization, if your library is a member of either. Both may have committee opportunities, events, or email lists that will help you connect with people in your broader geographic area.

A month or two after Sara started at her current university, she saw an announcement for a peer mentoring group from the center for the success of women faculty. Since librarians are considered faculty at the university, Sara was eligible to join. She met faculty from across campus, even from branch campuses, and was assigned a smaller group for peer mentoring. This mentoring was extremely informal, usually coffee dates where the five women shared successes, struggles, and mutual support. Sara got a better picture of what the frustrations were across campus, how the university operated, and what the working life of other faculty looked like.

When Tina started at the very large university, she answered a call for faculty senators. She knew little about the university and wasn't sure what a faculty senate did. Her idea was to say yes to the opportunities presented to her to see what she would like. It was yet another learning curve but attending senate meetings was a great way to learn how the university functioned as well as an opportunity to meet people.

See what's going outside of your normal work hours, too. Kathy said that was a big part of connecting to her campus:

> I went to some of the talks and the events they had in the evening, whether it was our speaker series or plays or whatever, concerts that the students were putting on, and I always encourage my new library faculty and staff to take advantage of what's available largely for free on campus … One of the things I always suggest to people is that they come back to campus on non-work hours, come back for a speaker, come back to see a play … I think coming to campus, even just walking through campus on a Saturday or Sunday afternoon, you get an understanding of what's going on in our student environment.

She also spoke about what that would mean at a public library:

> For a public library I think it would be attending some of the programming that you're not putting on, or going to a city council meeting, if that's the kind of thing that happens in your town, or the Rotary … It just depends where the environment is, but you have to be willing to put yourself out there to start to become familiar with it.

A new geographic area

One of Audrey's first steps after moving to a new location was to find out where she wanted to stop for coffee on the way to work.

> I've always moved from a different state or a country to start a new position, so there's a whole lot of co-orienting going on. I don't know where the Dunkin' Donuts on the way to work is, and if I don't have the coffee before I go into the work, then there aren't the questions [at work].

Moving to a new location isn't easy, especially when combined with starting a new job. Your new colleagues will likely be happy to share tips for whatever you need from a new doctor to the best ways to get around. It gives you an easy conversation starter: "Hello, are you from around here? Could I ask you where the …" Learning a new location can compound the new job brain fog so factor in a little extra of whatever helps you recuperate, be it more downtime or lots of exploring.

Finding your "third place" can help the new area feel more like home. Whether this is a religious or civic organization, a place where you can pursue a favorite hobby (such as a craft store or game shop), or an activity related to children or pets, finding that other outlet is like finding the third leg for a stool. Home, work, other. It can help with perspective.

Be aware of how often you mention how things were done in your old library

It is natural when you start at the new library to see everything in comparison to how your old library did it. It's also natural to want to share this with your new colleagues. A little of this is useful in helping your colleagues understand where you're coming from, what you know, and what's new to you. There is certainly the opportunity to share ideas from the old place that might work in the new. Try to not bring the old library up constantly though; even if the comparisons are going on in your mind, remember that you don't need to share everything with your new colleagues. The focus should be on learning the new place.

Questions for reflection

1. What reports or statistics are you most likely to use in your new job? Where do you go to run those reports or document those statistics?
2. What information will you be required to supply for the annual report?
3. Who has worked at your new library the longest?
4. What committees could you join?
5. Are there community clubs (like the Rotary Club, Chamber of Commerce, Elk's Lodge, Kiwanis, or Veterans of Foreign Wars) that could use library representation?
6. When the new job brain fog hits, what are three ideas for refreshing, calming, or energizing yourself?

6 Looking inward
Managing your emotions

Librarians can experience stress and diminished confidence when starting a new job. Some people feel overwhelmed, frustrated, disoriented, or defensive when they suddenly don't know how to do mundane tasks. Learn about this phenomenon and how to deal with it using concepts from psychology and pointers from the authors and other experienced librarians. This chapter uses the Social Readjustment Rating Scale, and the concepts of emotional differentiation and culture shock to help you cope. Learn tips on handling nerves and dealing with ambiguity. This chapter will help you put your past work experience in context for your new colleagues and deal with their assumptions about the library environment that you transitioned from. You'll also understand the challenges when moving between small and large libraries. If you experience impostor Syndrome, this chapter has guidance to identify and manage those feelings. Advice for finding support and building confidence is also provided. The chapter concludes with questions for reflection.

Introduction

The mid-career librarian is often confident in their skills. They have been in the field a few years, long enough to experience a problem, devise a plan, and see the resolution. Perhaps the mid-career librarian has been promoted and is seen by their colleagues as having specialized knowledge.

Likewise, a new MLIS graduate may see themselves as a model student. Perhaps they were top of their class or had a great internship where they gained valuable experience and are now ready to embark on their career path. They are confident in the new skills they have learned and are eager to put them in practice.

When the librarian, regardless of experience, then transitions to a new library, they may find their confidence unexpectedly eroded. No longer are they the go-to person for a solution. No longer do they know their job inside and out. They lack the institutional knowledge and savvy that their new colleagues have. They can no longer do their job automatically – they must think through how to approach things or ask to how to do basic tasks within the context of their new institution. Skills transfer, of course, but not all knowledge will.

Many of our interviewees talked about the disorientation they felt when they started on the reference desk at their new libraries. Anna told us about a colleague who would do a good-natured impression of her on the reference desk, because Anna would refer every question she received to her colleague when she first started. When Sonia started at an academic law library, she had to learn a whole new vocabulary before she could answer questions on the desk.

> When I moved here to law it was really [challenging] to learn new terminology. I mean new terms that I never even heard in English, my mother tongue is Spanish, and some of these terms I never even knew what they meant ... just to feel comfortable answering questions when, in a way at the beginning you don't even know what they are talking about.

Everyone who experiences this drop in confidence deals with it differently. Some people will feel unmoored, overwhelmed, or frustrated. Others will find themselves unexpectedly defensive and prickly when they need to ask questions or are questioned in turn by their new colleagues. Should you feel yourself growing defensive, try to take a moment to gather your thoughts and reframe your situation. The last thing you want is to lash out at well-meaning coworkers. Remind yourself that this is part of the adjustment process, and that you will regain your footing in a matter of months. Work on reframing the situation in your mind as an opportunity to learn. When you encounter a situation where you're unsure of your approach, consciously tell yourself that you are taking this opportunity to learn how to solve this type of problem. If you work at this, this can drastically change your attitude.

Some librarians will have no problem with this temporary erosion of their knowledge base. If that's you, fantastic! You may not find this chapter as applicable to your situation. Just bear this chapter in mind in case your feelings change. Many librarians, particularly those who pride themselves on their deep knowledge, may be frustrated or anxious when moving to their new library. This is completely normal, and blessedly temporary.

Audrey spoke about the toll that losing institutional knowledge can take on a new librarian:

> Lacking any institutional knowledge is just a real handicap, and it's not exactly something you can plug into your brain and download, it takes time. I completely understand where that lack of confidence is because you really can't answer those questions. But that's not a judgment on you, that is a reminder that you can't know everything all at once.

On stress and transitions

If you've gone through a job transition recently, you'll probably remember how stressful they can be. If it's been a while since you've changed jobs, you may be surprised by the amount of stress you experience. It's long been noted by psychiatrists that stress and career transition go hand in hand. In 1967, psychiatrists Holmes and Rahe published a foundational paper on the effect of life events, stress, and illness. They developed what they called the Social Readjustment Rating Scale and assigned points to various major life events, and then found if a subject had over 150 points in a single year, that person had a greater risk of hospitalization. If a person had over 300 points, the risk was compounded. In this study, a big job transition (labeled "business readjustment") was assigned 39 points. "Change to a different line of work" is 36 points, and "change in responsibilities at work" is 29. If you combine a career change with a relocation ("change in residence" 20 points) and a mortgage ("major mortgage" 32 points, "minor mortgage" 17 points), the stressful events literally add up. Though this paper is a few decades old, it is still regularly written about and cited and considered helpful for psychiatrists (Scully, Tosi, and Banning, 2000).

So, if you are feeling extra stress around your career transition, that is perfectly normal! If you find yourself experiencing many multiple stressful life events in the same year, take active steps to reduce your stress levels. Reach out to a friend, try meditation, or consider help from a trained professional. There is no reason to handle all of this stress on your own.

Knowing how you feel

Kashdan, Barrett, and McKnight wrote about a concept called emotional differentiation, ultimately saying that, "Those more adept in constructing granular, precise experiences will be better able to deal with them, no matter their intensity" (2015, p. 14). So, it is beneficial for librarians to take stock of their emotions and be honest with themselves about how they are doing in the midst of a career transition.

The concept of emotional differentiation means that the better you can pinpoint and describe what you are feeling, the better you will be at handling those emotions (Kashdan, Barrett, and McKnight, 2015). So, perhaps you acknowledge that you feel overwhelmed after your first shift at the desk. But consider, why do you feel that way? Are you anxious that you will not be able to rebuild the same kind of vast knowledge base that you had in her head at your previous job? Are you reacting to not knowing everything about your job inside and out? By being able to identify what exactly you are experiencing, you will be better able to process emotions and deal with any underlaying anxiety. Picture the trope of the therapist probing with "and how does that make you feel?"

Dealing with nerves

When Sara moved to Orlando to begin work at the University of Central Florida, she knew it would be a big change. Her previous professional library experience was at a small community college in a small town, so she was moving to a much larger institution as well as a much larger city. Because it was such a big change, she began to feel quite nervous about it, fearing that the experiences she had wouldn't adequately prepare her for this new environment. She was plagued by doubt. "What if I can't hack it? What if this is a mistake, and I've uprooted for nothing?"

It's normal to feel nervous about a big transition. Before you begin a new job, there's a lot that is unknowable. You won't know what your day-to-day will look like, if you'll get along with your colleagues, or even where you'll have lunch. All this uncertainty can make some people feel unmoored. There are steps you can take before you even leave your old job that will help calm the pre-move jitters. First, acknowledge how you feel and give yourself permission to be less than confident. If you are nervous, admitting it to yourself is a good start.

It is also important to talk to trusted friends or colleagues about how you're feeling. Sara mentioned her fears to a few friends and was given great advice and assurance. Her friends reminded her that no one is expected to know everything their first day on the job, and she shouldn't put so much pressure on herself. Your friends are likely to remind you of your past successes, or how you felt when you started the job you're leaving.

If you feel yourself becoming overwhelmed, take a step back and regroup. When we asked Ronit about advice for people undergoing a big library transition, she said that

> the biggest thing is to be kind to yourself. I know that sounds cliché, but it's really hard. Especially with our jobs, a lot of the time we help people and then send them on their way, and we never know if we provided the right resources, or if we just overloaded them with information, so for me always I find it very difficult to know whether or not I'm doing the right thing, whether I've done a good job. And especially when you're starting a new job, it's really hard to not get that kind of verbal reinforcement. So I'd definitely say that the biggest thing is to be kind to yourself, just do the best you can, I guess, and don't worry if you don't get a response.

Find something to look forward to in your move to a new environment. This could be something you're excited to leave behind, such as a particularly nasty commute, or maybe you're happy you'll never have to help someone figure out the library's printing system again. Also look for exciting things about your new location, like a new café near the library you'd like to stop by,

92 Looking inward

or a park you'd like to visit. You can train yourself to focus on these exciting aspects rather than the unknown or anxiety-inducing.

Next, find a coping strategy that works for you. Some people will get comfort from learning as much as possible about their new environment. They will read articles their new colleagues have written or take internet tours of their new neighborhood and plan for their first week of meals. However, others may find an onslaught of information overwhelming and prefer to learn things at a slower pace and discover things in person or through conversation. Neither method is inherently better, but one may be much better for you.

These are things you can begin doing before your job transition that will prepare you emotionally for a big shift.

The adjustment process

Challenges when moving between small and large libraries

Coordinating departments: One of the biggest challenges Sara faced moving from a small library to a large library was losing control over some processes. At a small library, Sara oversaw every step a book took in technical services, from ordering to getting on the shelf. If something needed to be changed, she didn't have to consult with different departments. She could unilaterally implement some changes or get input from her colleagues quite quickly and easily. Now, she only has control over a small section of the technical services process. Coordinating projects that involve multiple departments is a much bigger deal. She can't assign work to people who don't report to her, so she must approach the situation very differently than she did before.

Audrey experienced this loss of control when she moved from a small library to a large public library system, saying that she sometimes felt like she was "a cog – which there's pros and cons to … There were aspects that I didn't like not having control over."

Conversely, a librarian moving from a large library to a small library may find themselves taking on roles that were entirely different positions at their previous library. It's very likely that every librarian at a small library will take a shift at reference, regardless of department. They won't have as many colleagues to rely on and can see the gaps in their specialization or skills more clearly, and when problems arise, they may have little or no budget to implement solutions. Whether you're moving from large or a small library, dealing with new departments can introduce anxiety, confusion, and uncertainty.

Isolation: Working at a small library can make it feel like you're living on an island. When there aren't many librarians, there will be knowledge gaps, and librarians will have to look outside the library for answers. Librarians moving from a large to a small library may have to reach out to their consortia or ask questions on email lists more frequently than they have in the past. Compounding the isolation at small libraries is the difficulty of travel. With a small staff, it's harder to coordinate time off for conferences and such.

Librarians moving from large to small libraries may have to winnow down the number of conferences they attend.

You can combat isolation by finding new avenues to connect to other librarians. For example, are there local or semi-local conferences or seminars that you can attend more easily than national conferences? Can you create an informal group for local librarians? If you are feeling isolated, chances are other librarians in neighboring towns do too. Find email lists and online discussion platforms that will keep you in the loop and connected. Join or pursue new avenues of participation with professional organizations; take advantage of those ready-made communities.

Involvement/non-involvement: A librarian moving from a small to large library will be surprised at how little they know about happenings in other parts of the library. At a small library, it's common for all librarians to be involved to some degree in everything that's happening. At a large library, there may be entire departments that rarely interact. A librarian moving from large to small may be surprised at the number of meetings and activities that require their involvement. At many small libraries, every librarian does reference, instruction, and collection development, and all these topics may be covered at one general librarian meeting. The librarian will likely be involved in discussions about topics that are well beyond their area of expertise.

Dealing with ambiguity

Frequently, a librarian moving into a new job will find that a lot of aspects of their position are up in the air or unresolved. When libraries post an opening, that is an opportunity for them to reassess how things are run. Often, that means realigning assignments and priorities, and there can be room for variation within the position. When the librarian is hired, a lot of the job may depend on their skills and interests.

In addition to ambiguity within job tasks, there's also a lot that's unknown about the new environment. A new librarian may find themselves asking who they can rely on for a straight answer and who will answer questions without judgment.

So how can you manage this ambiguity? Well, a large part of it is being open to change, both in circumstance and in expectation. You need to be flexible and go in with few expectations of what your new job will look like. It's also important for you to be honest with your new colleagues and supervisor about where your interests lie. The interview process is a great opportunity to ask clarifying questions about what the job will look like, or which parts of it are negotiable.

A big part of ambiguity is learning how to cope with its existence. You will not be able to dissolve all of it right away. When Tina was hired at the authors' current institution, she had the same job title and responsibilities as another librarian. It took a lot of time and discussion to sort out who would take over which tasks. She had to accept that a certain level of ambiguity would be there for as long as it took for these discussions to play out. She had to consciously tell herself to let go of some of the little details that she wanted to be settled immediately. Fortunately, she knew she was in a good library environment where she was free to voice her concerns and opinions. If you're coming from a toxic work environment, it can be particularly difficult to deal with this kind of ambiguity, as you'll have to trust that your colleagues have good intentions.

Culture shock

Sara was surprised by the amount of culture shock she felt when she began her new job. Because she had previously worked abroad, she had experience with culture shock and was able to contextualize her emotions. This was particularly helpful, as her knowledge of the culture shock curve led her to anticipate emotional swings as she grew accustomed to her new surroundings.

The culture shock "U-Curve Hypothesis" was created to explain the various emotions one feels when entering a new culture (Gullahorn and Gullahorn, 1963). It's a graph of the feelings someone experiencing culture shock goes through, shaped like the letter "U." When someone moves to a new culture, they are at the start of the U, initially feel elation, or something similar. Everything is new and exciting – even exotic! There are new restaurants to try, new parks to visit. Nothing is boring or mundane. Then, as familiarity sets in, people begin to feel irritation and annoyance. Problems pop up, and they don't know how to solve them. Or perhaps the bureaucracy takes on new, unexpected forms. People begin to miss their old culture and yearn for familiar foods or circumstances. This downward trajectory continues for a while, represented by the lowest point of the U. Eventually, the new culture begins to feel familiar. As people begin to adjust to their new environment, they may start to feel like they belong, and develop confidence, and they begin to feel good again.

This U-curve maps very well to job transitions. At first, a new job is full of excitement and possibility. A librarian moving into a new position may find themselves thinking of their most-hated tasks and say, "I'll never have to do that again!" or happy to move on from a particularly difficult colleague. A new position offers new opportunities, new colleagues, and maybe even a new café to stop by in the mornings. As the novelty wears off, the new librarian may start to feel overwhelmed, or aggravated that tasks are taking longer to accomplish in this new environment. They may have their confidence shaken by lack of encyclopedic knowledge and be frustrated at how often they need to look things up. Perhaps they miss their old coworkers and old routines. Then, as they become more familiar with their new job, they will find themselves able to answer questions on the fly, or have the opportunity to run a few meetings, and will feel a bit more confident and secure in this new position.

Figure 6.1 is an adapted library version of the U-curve, with additional curves to demonstrate that it can occasionally be a bumpy transition:

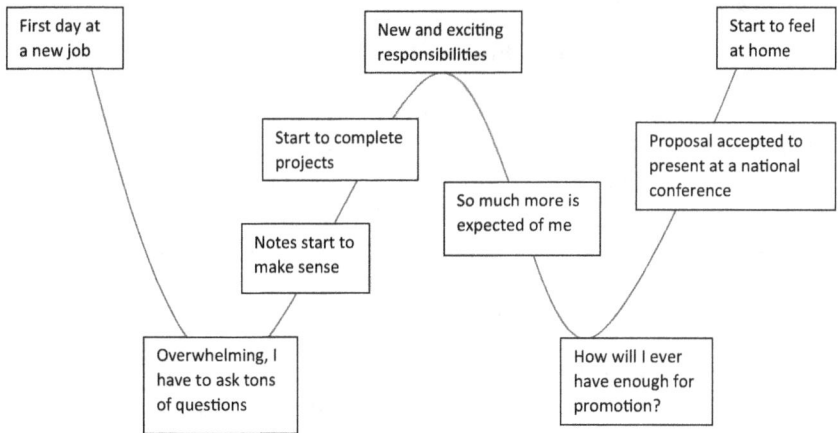

Figure 6.1 Adapted U curve.

It's important for librarians to know that a job adjustment takes time, and they need to push past that first downturn. The new job starts in a honeymoon phase and then can take an emotional downturn, but that is perfectly normal. Within a few months, things will begin to feel familiar, and within a year a librarian can expect to feel confident in their new role.

Sara wasn't alone in feeling a measure of culture shock. Several of our interviewees had similar experiences: Fred said that

> coming into a large public library was a bit of a culture shock, because with all the paperwork and rules and regulations and this, that, and the other ... There what was the biggest factor of longevity I would say is having a very good supervisor, a supportive supervisor ... we had a very good collaborative relationship, plus she gave me tips about working within the bureaucracy.

Jodie also had this experience but felt more at home pretty quickly.

> After the first couple weeks when I was, okay this is culture shock, I really, really enjoyed it and it became a lot easier for me. It was just those first couple of weeks where it was, okay, this is really different ... you just have to get used to the new collection and a new method of doing things, and different policies. If you go in expecting it to be the same, you're going to be shocked.

She told us that if she had known this going in and kept an open mind, she doesn't think she would have experienced culture shock at all.

Putting your past in context

When a librarian moves to a different type or size of library, many of their new colleagues may quite literally not understand where they're coming from. For example, a public librarian moving to an academic library will need to recharacterize their past work or environment using academic jargon. When Tina went from a public library to a university, she found it helpful to think of the colleges within the university as analogous to branches within the public library system. The colleges are affiliated with the university, as branches in a public library system are, but they have their own budgets, personnel, and goals. But, of course, all of those goals relate back into the system's overarching goals.

As you begin to adjust your experience to the vocabulary of your new environment, you may begin to feel misunderstood. If you notice yourself feeling this way, talk to one of your mentors outside your new library. Someone outside the situation can help you get perspective and reassure you that this is part of the adjustment process.

Dealing with assumptions

New librarians will always find themselves dealing with assumptions about their previous employment that they find themselves having to clarify. For example, when Sara moved from a small library to a large library, her new staff assumed that she was already familiar with the ILS because she was moving within the state system. However, though she did use the same ILS, it was configured very differently, and her previous library didn't use all of the modules because the library was so small.

Assumptions go both ways on a personal level as well. There will be many things that you took for granted, or wouldn't have thought to ask about, that will be different at your new library. It's important to talk to your mentors, particularly your institutional mentor, to check your assumptions. In some cases, it might be good to run an email you're going to send to an internal email list past your institutional mentor to make sure that you've framed it correctly, and aren't assuming jargon or processes or accidentally stepping into a political issue.

Adjusting to the new culture

As you spend time at your job, you'll want to take note of what atmosphere your new library has. Some of this you can ascertain from the interview process, but keep in mind everyone is on their best behavior (usually!) during an interview. You can ask if people are open and welcoming at an interview, but rarely will you get an answer other than, "Oh yes! Everyone here is very friendly. We're a great team!" Once you're there, you'll want to feel out how relaxed thing are, or if there's more structure in some areas. For example, can you just drop by people's office when you have a question, or is the "corporate culture" more formal? Perhaps it's better to email first and make an appointment to discuss something. Does everyone arrive at the same time every day? Do you need to be there at a certain time on the dot? Will people notice and comment if you're a few minutes late? At some libraries, being late is a big faux pas, but at others, people will not even notice.

Begin to explore how open people are to working together on projects. Is this a genuinely nice team of librarians? Or are there people who can be a bit backbiting? If you have an institutional mentor who is forthcoming, ask them for their perspective. At many places, you'll find a mix of people, some of whom are genuinely helpful and a few of whom are best avoided.

Aside from the culture of the place, you'll likely find yourself surrounded by new acronyms. It seems libraries, no matter where you are, love acronyms! Sometimes you feel like you don't even speak the same language. At UCF (the University of Central Florida), we're an ASERL (Association of Southeast Research Libraries) institution. We belong to the SUS (State University System), and some decisions are made by CSUL (Council of State University Libraries). We are serviced by FALSC (the Florida Academic Library Services Cooperative), which long-time librarians may occasionally refer to by either of their previous names: FLVC (Florida Virtual Campus) or FCLA (Florida Center for Library Automation). We have monthly meetings run by FAC (Faculty Advisory Committee); DAG (the Director's Advisory Group) runs the social events and takes up staff concerns; and PDRA (Professional Development Research Award) offers an opportunity for research funding. This doesn't even touch on professional organization acronyms: PLA, ALA, FLA, ALCTS, RUSA, YALSA, etc. It's enough to make you want to pull your hair out! A new librarian can easily get overwhelmed by all of this or get discouraged and feel like they have no clue what's going on. Going in, be aware that there will be many different acronyms that will make no sense to you in your first month or so. Write down every acronym that is new to you and look them up. You may want to dedicate a separate notebook to this task, and you can develop a glossary of terms specific to your new library or role. This will help you build your confidence back up, and as you decode what people are discussing in meetings you'll eventually feel like you belong.

Impostor syndrome

Some lucky librarians will be completely immune to impostor syndrome and wonder why on Earth objectively qualified people would think themselves unworthy. For the rest of us, it's important to acknowledge it and deal with it.

Clance and Imes identified what they termed "impostor phenomenon" back in 1978: "The term impostor phenomenon is used to designate an internal experience of intellectual phoniness which appears to be particularly prevalent and intense among a select sample of high achieving women" (p. 241). They went on to discuss how that manifests, saying: "Despite outstanding academic and professional accomplishments, women who experience the impostor phenomenon persist in believing that they are really not bright and have fooled anyone who thinks otherwise" (p. 241). According to their research, achievements did not do much to break down these feelings.

Since then, the impostor phenomenon, or impostor syndrome, has been written about extensively. Of course, though Clance and Imes initially wrote about it in the context of women's experiences, impostor syndrome can be experienced by anyone, regardless of gender.

Librarians transitioning to a new job are ripe for impostor syndrome to creep in. Perhaps new colleagues are not deferring to you because they don't know your experience or expertise. Your knowledge may be essentially wiped out as you start afresh, and you may find yourself feeling like you don't know as much as you thought you did. Those who have always felt confident may start to feel less so, and those making big career changes have the deck stacked against them in this regard.

Am I experiencing impostor syndrome?

If you begin to notice yourself thinking things like "why did they even hire me?" or feeling like you will be discovered as a fraud at any moment, you are likely experiencing impostor syndrome. Even if you aren't actively thinking this way, you may still be at risk.

Do any of the following statements resonate with you?

- I am going to be fired.
- I don't have what it takes to do this job.
- I don't know what I am doing.
- I am less competent than my colleagues.
- Everyone knows what they're doing except for me.

If any of these have popped up in your internal monologue, you may be going through a bout of impostor syndrome. This may be a flash in the pan, over as soon as you notice you're feeling this way, but if it persists, please consider talking to someone about it. If you let the feelings fester, they may grow. If you discuss them with someone you trust, you can begin to process these feelings and prune them away.

When you begin a new job, particularly if you are moving to a more complex institution, it feels like everyone else already knows everything, and you are playing catch up. This feeling is compounded if you are the only new person, and all of the other librarians have been in their positions for quite some time. It will often take months before you start to recognize the gaps in others' knowledge and appreciate your unique skills.

For example, when Sara was preparing to move to a very large research university from a community college, she was convinced all of her new colleagues would be at a completely different professional level than she was. She thought they would all know everything she knew, and she would be playing catch up from the moment she walked through the door. Over time, she began to notice that she had specialized knowledge that some of the other librarians didn't have. Subject librarians began treating her as the point person for clarification on eBook digital rights management (DRM) and user models, which she would happily explain. She realized that things she had thought everyone already knew were not, in fact, universal. Her expertise was validated. Take notice when your colleagues value your experience or point of view, and even write down when it happens if you're feeling particularly vulnerable. This can help you manage any impostor syndrome feelings as you look for more support.

Finding support

Impostor syndrome is not new and is not confined to any subject area or specialization. Therefore, many institutions may have resources in place for faculty or staff who are experiencing it. Even if they do not specifically call out impostor syndrome in their description, look for mentorship groups, meet ups, seminars, or other support services that connect you with people across your institution who may be feeling similarly. If your institution does not offer these types of resources, look outside to city or statewide library groups and mentorship opportunities. The more you are connected with others experiencing self-doubt, the more you will see that this is a common experience that you can overcome. One of the best ways to overcome impostor syndrome is to connect with mentors. There are many types of mentors explored in Chapter 4.

Andy offered some advice:

> Don't be afraid. If they want you, it's because they really want you. Plenty of people applied for that post, and you got through to interview and got offered the job. They see something in you that they like. Knock impostor syndrome on the head.

Sindhumathi Revuluri wrote a great advice piece in the *Chronicle of Higher Education* called "How to Overcome Impostor Syndrome" (2019). Her entire article is well worth reading, but some of her most helpful tips mainly boil down to resisting comparison to others. It is vital to remember that everyone has their own path and experiences, and that there is no true one-to-one comparison with another person. Focus on your own situation and experiences.

Something that really helped Sara build confidence in her new position was focusing on building her independence. Just a few months after she started, her supervisor left the country for a couple months. Sara was forced to make decisions about ongoing projects to keep things moving, and when things turned out well, she had to admit that she knew what she was doing. Her previous doubts about being ready for the transition from small library to huge academic research library began to fall away.

Interviewees comments on and experience with managing emotions

Pam experienced the worry of being new and unsure if she was doing the job well enough.

> you sort of have this fundamental insecurity: am I doing this well; am I doing this well enough; is there anybody sort of festering about something I haven't done; have I missed something? ... just talk with people about how things are working and just get that reassurance, those checks to make sure that you are doing everything that's required. So, I guess for me, the points where I would think, oh hey, I am sort of starting to get the hang of this – because people would either ask me a question that would indicate they had confidence in what I was doing or they would agree with a suggestion I'd made, and I'd think, yep, I've got this.

Sonia expresses confidence in people's abilities, even if they lack it themselves.

> But I was reading a lot about this impostor syndrome. So, I mean, I don't think people need to be afraid of jumping into an opportunity when you don't know something ... I would suggest anyone just to take an opportunity and go for it.

Throughout our conversation with Sonia, she stated her strong belief that people are capable of learning whatever they need to.

Jenn:

> Somebody told me I was brave, and I kind of laughed at them because I'm so scared of so many things. But to be able to take that leap of faith and just trust that it will work is a big deal.

Jinnie:

> I always feel like I'm new. If I knew everything, A) what would be the challenge in even having a new job, and B) there's no way I could know everything, it's an unrealistic expectation. That's not to say I'm not plagued with impostor syndrome constantly about my own capabilities on what [jobs] I would be eligible for.

Jodie:

I always asked [the other library CEOs] … "what do you wish you knew when you first became a CEO?" And every single one of them was like, "I had no clue what I was getting into, I thought I was ready and I wasn't" or a version of that … So if these CEOs of these huge libraries are saying this, I'm obviously not doing too bad.

Kady:

I would say you can't beat yourself up for not knowing something that you've never experienced before.

Deb:

You have those days that you don't feel like you're catching on, but you also have those days that are just great. So, you just have to press on. Chances are if you don't have that erosion of confidence, you're not learning anything.

Audrey:

My mom always says give something three months before you even give it a beginning judgment, which I think has served me well. If you're there for a year and you think you're going to die, go, get out. If you're there for a year and you think "ok this is getting a little bit better, I think next year at this time I will feel more confident and fulfilled, and like I'm serving this community the way I need to be serving it and also growing in my career," then stay. But don't throw good time after bad. Don't be afraid to move on.

Lisa:

Oh my gosh, impostor syndrome is real. I am a former librarian with a masters, MLIS. I work with people now who have PhDs. It's hard, it's hard to be in that sort of environment. I struggle with that a lot because I don't have a PhD, everyone here has a PhD, mostly … Yeah, that's real. I don't even know how to answer that. You're not the only one! Everyone feels like that. I think even the PhDs feel like that. I don't know how we overcome that. I'm not above asking stupid questions, but it's hard to do that when you're new, because you don't want people to know you don't know something. So, I guess it goes back to finding those people, finding your safe people, your mentor people who you can ask stupid questions of, and just realizing that you're not alone, nobody really knows what they're doing. Other people are just better at hiding it.

Questions for reflection

1. How do you feel about your job transition? What are you looking forward to? What is making you anxious?
2. Have you experienced culture shock before? Do you think you'll experience it in this new environment?
3. Are there details about your new job that still need to be ironed out?
4. What are assumptions you're making about your new library? Are any of them unfounded?
5. Have you experienced impostor syndrome? Have you experienced burnout? Do you think you'll recognize the symptoms if you start to experience either of them?

References

Clance, P. R., & Imes, S. A. (1978). The Impostor Phenomenon in High Achieving Women: Dynamics and Therapeutic Intervention. *Psychotherapy: Theory, Research & Practice*, 15(3), 241–247. https://doi.org/10.1037/h0086006

Gullahorn, J. T. & Gullahorn, J. E. (1963). An Extension of the U-Curve Hypothesis. *Journal of Social Issues*, 19(3), 33–47. https://doi.org/10.1111/j.1540-4560.1963.tb00447.x

Holmes, T. H., & Rahe, R. H. (1967). The Social Readjustment Rating Scale. *Journal of Psychosomatic Research*, 11(2), 213–218. https://doi.org/10.1016/0022-3999(67)90010-4

Kashdan, T. B., Barrett, L. F., & McKnight, P. E. (2015). Unpacking Emotion Differentiation: Transforming Unpleasant Experience by Perceiving Distinctions in Negativity. *Current Directions in Psychological Science*, 24(1), 10–16. https://doi.org/10.1177/0963721414550708

Revuluri, S. (2019). How to Overcome Impostor Syndrome: Scholars of all Ages Wrestle with Feelings of "Intellectual Phoniness." So How Do You Get over It? *The Chronicle of Higher Education*, 17, 31. www.chronicle.com/article/How-to-Overcome-Impostor/244700

Scully, J. A., Tosi, H., & Banning, K. (2000). Life Event Checklists: Revisiting the Social Readjustment Rating Scale after 30 years. *Educational and Psychological Measurement*, 60(6), 864–876. https://doi.org/10.1177/00131640021970952

7 Publishing, presenting, and conferencing

This chapter presents guidance and support for the librarian in a new environment who needs to figure out scholarship, conference attendance, doing presentations, writing, and publishing. Is scholarship required by your new library? What funding and leave time are provided? Find conferences in your area of librarianship. Learn the benefits of giving presentations. The chapter gives advice on finding a co-presenter, and dealing with stage-fright or nerves. This chapter helps librarians to understand the influence of library size, staffing needs, and job scope. For the librarian who isn't ready to present, this chapter offers other ways to get involved at conferences, such as doing a poster session, volunteering, moderating a panel discussion, or doing a lightning round. This chapter then discusses different types of writing and publishing; and what is scholarship versus service or making a name for yourself. There are numerous suggestions for finding a topic for your presentation or writing follow. Finally, the authors suggest that you pursue these professional development areas even if your current job doesn't require it. You don't know what you'll need in a job 5, 10, or 20 years from now, so lay the groundwork for your future self. The chapter concludes with questions for reflection.

Introduction

It is jolting to make a move within one's profession and then find that an entire area of job performance is viewed completely differently. Scholarship is such an area. The requirements, opportunities, and funding for scholarship can vary drastically between types and sizes of libraries. Even within academia, there are numerous variations. The impact of size may be especially unexpected, such as having fewer colleagues who can cover for an absence or if narrowed job scope makes fewer conference sessions relevant. The amount of funding available from one's institution might be the most variable factor of all. We will discuss the range of variation so that the librarian seeking a change isn't taken by surprise and can make an informed decision.

If the expectation to publish and present is new, it can be difficult to know where and how to start. We will offer pointers for coming up with topics and collaborators as well as ways to get your feet wet before jumping in to a full-length conference presentation or journal article.

Whether you have to publish and present as part of your new job duties or because you're trying to meet colleagues and build a name, both options are great ways to learn, grow, and share. This chapter will help identify opportunities and develop ideas for topics. Then we'll discuss getting to the conference (either physically or virtually) and what to do once there.

Scholarship and research

What are scholarship and research? As we touched on in Chapter 3, this category includes a variety of ways that the librarian can contribute to the professional body of knowledge, such as writing articles and case studies for scholarly journals, or books and book chapters. This category also includes doing presentations, posters, workshops, and panel discussions at conferences or webinars. Brief publications such as news items or reports of conference presentations are usually considered to be service. Short book reviews may also be service while longer, analytical reviews may fall into the research and creative category. Likewise with bibliographies.

What is required

What, if any, amount of scholarship is required by your job? For instance, at the very large Florida university, the authors have a percentage of their time dedicated to "research and creative activities," which includes such activities as writing articles for scholarly journals and developing and giving presentations at library conferences (and writing career guides for librarians!) The authors have heard of 10% of a librarian's time allocated to scholarship at tenure-granting academics or 5% at their own institution where librarians are not eligible for tenure. At some institutions, there may be no requirement for scholarship, but some amount of work time devoted to it may be recognized as suitable, beneficial professional conduct. At other institutions, the librarian may have to pursue such activities on their own time.

If you're thinking about moving to an institution where scholarship is required and that's new for you, it's time to learn about the options to see if this is something you will enjoy and be able to do. Read the professional literature and consider if that's something you want to contribute to. Reach out to your professional communities and ask other librarians about their experiences publishing and presenting.

If you're thinking about moving to an institution where scholarship isn't required and that's new for you, consider how or if you want to continue pursuing those activities on your own time. You may be happy to put that aside and focus on the day-to-day work of librarianship.

What is funded and given leave time

The amount of monetary support given to librarians for scholarship varies greatly between institutions. These funds could support travel and related costs necessary to do research or to attend conferences or registration fees for conferences. Budget, the value placed on these activities, and the number of librarians who request funding all play a role. The librarian should be prepared to justify the benefit of their request and to prioritize them. If requests aren't fully funded, how much are you willing and able to pay out of pocket?

The other variable is how much leave time a librarian gets to pursue scholarship. You must factor in not only the policy at the library but also the potential for an overload of work awaiting your return. Unless you're on a formal leave where it's stipulated that you don't do your normal job, it's not uncommon for conference-goers, for example, to be fielding work emails during breaks and at the end of the day.

Conferences and presenting

Perhaps obviously, there are lots of library-oriented conferences. Most occur in a physical destination, but some are online-only, where both presenters and attendees are participating from home or office. Some conferences combine elements of both, where perhaps all presentations and many attendees are in one physical space but some presentations are broadcast online, whether freely available or fee-based access. So even if you are unable to physically attend a conference, you may be able to watch selected conference speakers for free at your desk.

You'll also want to talk with your supervisor about how much leave is given for conference attendance, how much is typically covered by professional development funds, how travel requests are made, and whether doing a conference presentation or serving on a conference committee is a prerequisite. Budgets and professional leave vary greatly between libraries so make no assumptions. If your library isn't able to cover all of your desired conferences each year, consider which is the priority and how much, if any, you're willing and able to supplement. Finally, be prepared to explain why each conference will be beneficial for you to attend and what benefit you can bring back to the library.

If you're moving to a new location or new type of library, you may not be familiar with the most relevant conferences. Certainly, ask your new colleagues which conferences they find most useful. (While you're at it, ask which email lists they like.) However, colleagues aren't your only source. For solo librarians, your boss or institution may be able to tell you which conferences your predecessor attended. Email lists may provide good options. If you are involved with the library ILS, there is likely a conference specific to that product (or family of products). This is true of some other library products, too, often electronic resource related such as discovery layers and online media. If you work closely with vendors, it is worth asking those sales representatives which conferences their company participates in. Consortia often have general meetings (which may or may not be called conferences) where member librarians can offer a presentation. There are a range of conferences for different types of libraries and librarians, such as the Public Library Association (PLA) conference and the Electronic Resources & Libraries (ER&L) Conference. Of course, regional, state/provincial, national, and international conferences abound. However, it is surprisingly difficult to find a comprehensive list of library and information science conferences. The following sites may be useful:

- Library Conference Planner, maintained by Douglas Hasty: http://lcp.douglashasty.com/index.html
- Events Calendar from Information Today: www.infotoday.com/calendar.asp
- Against the Grain Conferences, Meetings, and Webinars (free email sign-up) – this is a publication from the group that puts on the Charleston Conference on Library Acquisitions: https://against-the-grain.com/. Navigate to the conference, meetings, and webinars section and/or sign up for the daily emails; once per week, they send an email listing conferences, meetings, etc.

Benefits of giving conference presentations

Though presentations can involve a lot of time and preparation, they can do a lot for your career. If you're moving into a library that requires scholarship, you may not have a choice as to whether or not to present. However, even if it's not required, presenting is a valuable skill that can help you make a name for yourself. Your name will go into the conference program, along with an abstract of your presentation, and you may be able to contribute a paper to the conference proceedings. You're now part of the public record of that conference, and when other librarians are searching for someone knowledgeable on your topic you may come up in their results.

Even if you have a lot of years of experience in the field, librarians who haven't ever worked with you won't know unless you put yourself out there. Presenting is a way for you to publicly demonstrate your expertise. Librarians who attend your sessions may ask you questions after, or run into you later in the conference and want to discuss points you've made.

Finding a co-presenter

If you're new to presenting, it may be less intimidating to have a co-presenter or two. There may be an easy choice if you want to present about a project that you worked on with one or more colleagues. If you handled the project on your own, you still have a couple of options. First, consider who was heavily impacted by the project; would their comments about the impact or scope of the project be a meaningful addition? For instance, if you created programming for children with sensory issues, could an articulate parent participate in the presentation by explaining the need and benefit?

Another way to find co-presenters is to reach out to people you know in professional associations or from email discussion lists, thinking of those who have commented about the desired presentation topic. This can be a little riskier because you have less knowledge about the person's work habits but with the risk comes the possibility of forming a stronger bond with these colleagues.

Lastly, remember that there are even options if people are willing to co-develop the presentation but cannot attend the conference with you. Depending on the capabilities of the conference hall, they may be able to participate via Skype or other call-in software. There is an option in PowerPoint to record voice-overs to accompany multiple slides. The presenter in the room simply advances the slide to start the voice-over. Tina has participated in presentations where co-presenters used both of these methods and they worked. However, we recommend having a print copy of your co-presenter's comments as a backup. Actually, you may want to have a print copy of your comments as well – sometimes technology will fail.

Dealing with nerves or stage fright

It's entirely understandable to have stage fright before and while you're giving a presentation. It happens to many people. Here are some ways to reduce your nervousness.

First, remember that you have something of value to share. It's great that you have this opportunity to share stuff with your peers. Remember those two positive things; it's easy to lose sight of them in the busyness of a conference. Sharing knowledge is what our profession is about so these are both significant.

Next, remember that your presentation likely won't be of value to every single librarian in the room and that's completely normal. You've probably been to presentations that just weren't on target for you; it happens. Remember that you're doing your presentation for the people who *are* valuing the content. Some people – you can't always tell who – are hanging on your every word and really need to know this stuff. Their interest may not be evident from their posture or their expression. It might be someone staring at you and it might be someone else who's madly typing on their laptop and never even looks up. Just have faith that they're there and do the presentation for them.

As you talk, let your eyes move around the room at a comfortable rate. You'll see some people who are looking at you with friendly expressions. Let your eyes go to them when you look to the audience. (Once you realize the value of friendly faces in the audience, you'll always make the effort to be one of them, forever afterward.) Friendly faces are reassuring so go ahead and accept that reassurance (Ford, 2019).

There's a tendency to talk quickly when you're nervous. Try to speak a little slower than your normal speech. It's good to pause between sentences and take a breath or have a sip of water. Remember that people are learning from you and they need time to absorb what you're saying, so a gentle pace is easier on them, too (Ford, 2019).

You'll likely feel more confident if you know your presentation inside and out so take plenty of time to rehearse prior to the conference. Try rehearsing in front of a mirror and practice looking up from your notes and making eye contact. Time yourself and adjust your presentation if need be. If it helps you, make notes within your presentations to remind yourself to look up at the audience, to pause, to breathe.

If people ask questions that you can't answer, simply acknowledge it, whether due to not knowing or being unable to remember. If it's something that you can readily ascertain after the presentation or after the conference, offer to get back to the questioner. Ask them to provide their contact information afterward. If the question isn't within the realm of your work, simply say that you don't know; if you like, you can ask if anyone else in the room knows the answer, but you should also feel comfortable continuing to respond to questions about your presentation rather than getting pulled off course.

The impact of size

Are there enough staff to cover if you're out of the office? When Sara was at the small community college, very limited travel funds were available for conference attendance. Even more critically, the staff was so small that very limited amounts of leave could be granted for professional travel in order to maintain sufficient coverage for library services. One of the benefits of moving to a larger institution is having more colleagues available as potential collaborators or co-presenters. Moving from an independent library to one that is part of a consortia presents similar possibilities.

A change in job scope has an impact on your conferencing and professional development activities as well as your daily work. When Tina worked at the small university, most technical services topics were very relevant to her job. Any conference that she attended typically offered more pertinent presentations than she could possibly get to. When she moved to the very large university, the scope of her job narrowed. Whole areas became someone else's responsibility. Presentations that would have been de rigueur were suddenly just curiosities. Vendors that she had made a point of talking with were no longer part of her orbit. Whether your job scope has narrowed or expanded, you may need to take a fresh look at planning your conference attendance. Does the general conference still offer enough targeted material for your specialty? Will the specialized conference be too narrow to be a worthy part of a tight budget?

Not ready to present? Ways to get your feet wet

Poster sessions

Poster sessions at conferences are a great way to dip your toe in the conference arena because you get to do most of the work out of the spotlight and avoid those public speaking jitters. Many conferences will have an open session where the poster creators are encouraged to stand by their posters and answer questions from attendees, but the atmosphere tends to be casual and the interactions are usually one-on-one or in very small groups.

The poster itself might depict a project, workflow innovation, or result of research. If you're not artistic, having creative, visually attuned friends or colleagues give feedback is very helpful. The poster should also be designed for all elements to be readable to those standing a few feet away. Each conference typically provides requirements or guidelines for size and print resolution as well as whether print or electronic or both are expected. If the library or broader institution doesn't offer a free printing option, the librarian has numerous options, from office supply stores to online printing service. In addition to paper, there are also online sources for printing custom works on fabric, such as Spoonflower and Vistaprint. Fabric posters are lightweight and very convenient to fold and pack, much more so than a poster-sized paper document.

Volunteer opportunities at conferences

Many conferences present opportunities for volunteers to perform functions such as publicizing the event; introducing speakers; working at the registration desk; helping with local arrangements; and more. The goal of this chapter is to get you to the conference. So, look for volunteer opportunities that occur, at least in part, during the conference. (Of course, you'll need to ascertain from your supervisor whether you can get leave time for this and if travel, housing, or other costs will be covered by the library.)

Once you've secured your attendance, find presentations that are of interest. Focus on those given by librarians; famous authors are interesting but other librarians are likely more relatable. Attend the presentations and watch with an eye toward how the actual presenting happens. Can you pick up any ideas for how the presenter engages the audience, how they frame their topic, how they handle questions? Are their presentation materials clear and easy to see? This is an opportunity to learn both from the content of the presentation as well as from the presenter's technique. Also notice the audience and register what seems normal or average for how attentive people are. This can help reassure you that your audience is receiving you in a typical way.

Be sure to talk with other volunteers. Ask about what kinds of participation has been meaningful to them. This may show you further opportunities to get involved.

Another form of volunteering at conferences involves serving on a committee that is meeting at the conference (and may have nothing to do with the actual running of the conference). For instance, Sara has served on committees that select the winners for various book awards. In addition to online meetings throughout the year, they also meet at ALA Midwinter Conference (caveat: the Midwinter Conference is being discontinued and it's not wholly clear what, if anything, will take its place). Tina has done a similar activity with a technical services committee that is part of what is currently called ALCTS (Association for Library Collections and Technical Services), a division of ALA. These committees have the benefit of providing a like-minded group of colleagues who you may not have met otherwise. These people could be naturals for future co-presenters or co-authors so pay attention to whose comments and behavior is appealing to you. Depending on your library's budget and policies, committee service may provide you at least some funding to attend the conference.

Lightning rounds

Lightning rounds can take a variety of formats. One typical example is that each presenter has 10 or 15 minutes to address their topic. If you're not up for a full-length presentation or you're not sure you have that much to say about a topic, this is a nice option. Usually, the presenter will speak for about two-thirds of the time and the remainder is for questions and answers. Another variant of the lightning round is when the presenter has a very limited amount of time to talk about a specific number of PowerPoint (or other presentation software) slides. One example of this is PechaKucha where the presenter has 20 seconds each for 20 slides, but there are numerous variations on the theme (PechaKucha, 2020). A shorter presentation may be less intimidating in terms of how long you're in front of the audience, but bear in mind that it often doesn't take less time to create – being concise takes a lot of effort!

Moderating or speaking in a panel discussion

A final option for dipping your toes into presenting is being a moderator for a panel discussion or participating as one of the panelists. Moderating can take the form of asking the panelists a list of prepared questions and then calling on audience members who have questions. Moderating may also take the form of guiding the panelists through a conversation about the presentation topic. Being a panelist would involve being one of those fielding questions or having a conversation with others in front of an audience. These involve less speaking time overall but often require more ability to speak extemporaneously and to deal with the unexpected.

Writing and publishing

This concept includes news items designed for colleagues and/or patrons; peer-reviewed, research-based articles destined for library and information science journals; reviews; how-to-do-it articles for professional journals; conference reports; and edited works. Writing for a professional newsletter, be it for your library, consortium, local association, etc., both establishes you as a writer with professional interests and gets your name "out there" as an active participant in the field. It shows that you have potential as a researcher (if you're thinking of going to a position that requires such) or could pitch in with marketing or publicity. Nearly any library organization and some conferences will put out publications of various types and be in need of writers.

For those needing to pursue academic scholarship, there is a scale of scholarliness, if you will. Brief publications such as news items, short book reviews and bibliographies, program summaries, and reports of conference presentations are usually considered to be service in the academic realm. But they still show professional engagement and provide evidence that the librarian can write and has future potential to do more. Longer, analytical book reviews and more detailed bibliographies may qualify as scholarly publishing.

Scholarly articles

Publishing in a peer-reviewed journal can seem intimidating, but like any other endeavor, it just requires getting started and figuring out the process as you go. Colleagues who have already been through the process are a good source of advice and encouragement, too. The journals themselves provide a lot of information. Identify a few within your specialty. Look at the "about" section and you should find a statement on the scope of the journal, i.e. what subject matters it covers. Read or at least closely scan a lot of articles to get a feel for their structure, tone, and content. Typical topics might be a study that the author conducted, or a discussion of a project undertaken. Notice the article's component parts and the order that they're in. These tend to be standard. Scholarly articles have a structure that can help guide your writing. Notice the tone, which will be formal and generally solely in the third person. Finally, notice the list of works cited; you're contributing to the scholarly conversation of the field and building on previous scholarship is an expected part of any such article.

To find out how to submit an article, see the journal's "about" section again. There is generally a page called something like "instructions for authors." This should tell you if the journal accepts submissions of unsolicited articles or wants brief proposals first. Another option is to watch the email lists for calls for proposals/submissions. Sometimes journals plan special issues dedicated to one topic, and they'll publicize this in advance to ensure they receive appropriate submissions.

Once you've made your submission, be prepared to wait. Turnaround times vary greatly and are no indication of either success or rejection. You may get a provisional acceptance, pending suggested edits, which may be minor or major. There are nearly always revisions and edits. If you have submitted to a peer-reviewed article, you'll get anonymous feedback from the peer-reviewers in addition to the editor. It can be a lengthy process of back-and-forth, but your article should emerge stronger for the outside input. Of course, don't take criticisms personally; you may agree or not with the comments but keep your focus on improving the article. Likewise, if your submission is rejected, don't take it personally. Look at your list of journals that publish on your topic and try again.

Blogging

Options for blogging may be obvious: create your own blog or contribute to another blog, be it someone else's, the library's, or another organization's. Below are a variety of library blogs. One is by a sole author; most have multiple contributors.

- Scholarly Kitchen: https://scholarlykitchen.sspnet.org/ (a wide variety of contributors, under the auspices of the Society for Scholarly Publishing).
- In the Library With the Lead Pipe: www.inthelibrarywiththeleadpipe.org/ (formerly a blog; now an online-only open access journal, not affiliated with an organization).
- ACRLog: https://acrlog.org/ (the blog of the Association for College and Research Libraries).
- Musings about Librarianship: http://musingsaboutlibrarianship.blogspot.com/ (an independent blog by Aaron Tay, a librarian in Singapore).
- Blogs and other publications from the Toronto Public Library: www.torontopubliclibrary.ca/blogs-publications/ (many departments and perspectives are addressed here).

Finding a topic

It's easy for librarians to think that the projects they've implemented are just something everyone already knows and not worth sharing in-depth. This thinking can stymie someone who is faced with presenting at conferences or writing for the profession: "What is there to say about this? Everything I did was just common sense." But it's only common sense if one had the experience of implementing the project. To outsiders, it's likely not simple or straightforward; other librarians may be entirely new to this realm of librarianship. Breaking a project down into steps, roadblocks, options, and solutions is one way to develop a "how-I-did-it" article or presentation.

Here are other some ideas for generating topics. Think of your various work assignments, their component parts, and the steps you took to implement or plan for a project. What was hard to figure out? What was an unusual path to take? What solved a problem? What do your colleagues, staff, or patrons absolutely love? Have you had success dealing with challenging populations? Have you formed a beneficial partnership with a community group? Maybe you developed a program or service that appeals to some hard-to-reach community segment. Have you collected data or statistics about a specific area over time (circulation, usage, budget, etc.?) Did that data lead you or your department to take some actions? And what about the data subsequently? Your numbers might tell a good story. All of these are potential topics.

Think of your background. Do you have uncommon knowledge or experience that might help others? Maybe you had a previous career that has been useful in your library life. Think of your skills and knowledge. What do people come to you for help with? What kinds of things are you good at – especially things that seem to frustrate or confuse others? Do you understand the latest cool free web service; bookkeeping concepts; space-planning; or how to write disaster plans? Maybe you developed successful craft or makerspace projects or figured out a clever way to get these things funded. These are things you can tell others about.

Tina often thinks of a colleague who is talented with PowerPoint and used it to design a jaw-dropping poster presentation. When Tina suggested the colleague offer a conference presentation or workshop of tips on how to do this, the colleague responded that it was no big deal, it was just a little thing she really liked to do. Tina knows it is a big deal though – making a compelling, appealing poster isn't easy or fun for everyone – and many people would be grateful to learn even a few tips.

Don't overlook what you could share and don't think that everyone knows what you know, even if you're early in your career or new to your environment. If you've had a talk accepted at a conference, or you've been asked to write a chapter or article on a topic, trust that people want to hear what you have to say.

No thanks, I'll never need to do any of this!

Unless you're very, very near to retirement, you can't be certain what you'll need in a job in five, ten, 20, or more years from now. Your wonderful boss could move on and be replaced by someone not to your liking. Family changes could force you to relocate. Lay-offs and downsizing impact even those in the organization who keep their jobs. You might change: you could get bored, become intrigued with a new area in the field, decide to walk through an unexpected open door, get an urge to move, or simply gain the confidence to pursue library work that seems out of reach now. Lay the groundwork now for your future self.

When Sara was working at a community college library, she didn't have any scholarship requirement. She was able to attend one conference a year, but due to the timing and structure of professional development funding at the community college, she didn't know if she would be able to attend this conference until long after the deadline for presentations. Because of these two factors, she only presented at the conference one year, and didn't publish in the conference proceedings. Publishing seemed like too big of a headache for no benefit at her position. As a result, when she decided to start applying to universities, she felt she was at a disadvantage, as she had scant presentations on her résumé and no publications at all. Now, even though she was hired at a large university with that scholarship background, she needs to do extra work to get her scholarship ready for promotion. If she had taken it upon herself to do even one or two publications in the seven years that she was a community college librarian, she would be in a much better position for promotion. Small steps can add up over time! If you think there's even the slightest possibility you'll end up at a university that has a promotion process, look into publishing at least one article.

Interviewees' perspectives on publishing, presenting, and conferencing

Pam has combined the concepts of mentoring, conferencing, and networking:

> No, I've never had a specific mentor; I've just had people that I could – I've always been keen on networking generally, so tend to seize opportunities if I'm meeting with somebody, I'll always have a sort of list of issues I want to raise with them ... Like if I go to a conference, I'll try and find the people who are in sort of a similar situation and ask how do you do this, and what is your approach here, and such like. So I make my own mentoring opportunities, I suppose, rather than ... others that have been specifically arranged ... I always make sure I keep business cards and email addresses and just have people in the back of my mind. If I happen to have a particular issue, I might say, well, how do you ... deal with it? But mentoring is a very good way to transition between roles. That's certainly something I'd recommend if it's possible. And if not, create your own mentoring opportunities.

Marian has long utilized networking and conferencing:

> another thing ... that has helped me a lot is I'm a huge believer that you must belong to your professional association. So, your state association, your national association. But one of the reasons I could step into this particular job I have now is I was president of this state's library association in the past. I worked for a long time, many roles with the New Mexico Library Association ... So, over the time in doing that

I learned a lot about public libraries, I learned a lot about general academic libraries, and I kind of kept my hand in that way with other kinds of libraries, in being a part of the professional association. And when I go to conferences, if I go to a general conference like ALA or NMLA, I don't just go to sessions that are designed for my type of library. I go to other kinds of sessions that are tangentially associated with what I do. So if it's anything about kids, I might go to a public library youth services program, instead of a school library program, because I could learn something.

Fred:

My boss's boss, I started working in January, and she said, "the Public Library Association conference is coming up in March, and you're going." Because I had worked in public libraries in high school ... but not as a professional. So she said it's important to find out what goes on in public libraries across the country. So that was a positive thing, as well, that she took interest. "We're going to throw you right into this."

Jodie:

I'm a member of ALA, I'm a member of FLA ... I participated heavily in FAME. All of those helped because it exposes you to the outside world, and you know you're not alone.

Kady:

If you're looking at a time of transition, if you can afford to, attend ALA, or [a conference related to the type you want to move into]. Networking in those areas where people are already gathering ... In a conference setting, you're already here and you're probably bored between sessions [so talk and network with people].

Questions for reflection
1. Are you required to pursue scholarship in your new job? What counts as scholarship?
2. What are some conferences you could present or volunteer at?
3. Who would you like to present or write an article with?
4. What are your favorite library journals? What requirements do they have for submission?
5. What's a library-related topic you enjoy discussing, or that you feel isn't adequately covered in the literature? How could you move forward to share this with a broader audience?

References

Ford, A. (2019). Boost your public speaking skills: Tips for librarians on speaking confidently and effectively in front of others. *American Libraries*, 50(11–12), 46–51. https://americanlibrariesmagazine.org/2019/11/01/boost-your-public-speaking-skills/

PechaKucha. (2020). *About PechaKucha*. PechaKucha.com. www.pechakucha.com/about

Further reading

Markgren, S. & Eatman, T.A. (2013). *Career Q&A: A Librarian's Real-life, Practical Guide to Managing a Successful Career*. Medford, NY: Information Today.

8 Tying it all together

The authors summarize the contents of this book, which provides support and guidance for librarians moving to different size or type of library. There is a discussion of the current state of libraries, including politics; budget; high demand on library services; libraries reinventing themselves to provide new services and prove their ROI (return on investment); issues surrounding Open Access and journal subscription models; and the challenge of dealing with homelessness, mental health issues, poverty, and similar challenges in the community. The current impact of COVID-19 and potential future fallout are discussed. The authors offer ways to monitor library trends and forecasts to benefit your career. They consider what the future holds for libraries in the area of funding; library associations; professional development costs; new technologies and formats that libraries will adopt; partnerships with external entities such as local government or postal or delivery services; patron privacy; and the future of the integrated library system. The chapter gives encouragement to find your support system, care for yourself, and push beyond your comfort zone. There is a list of characteristics that may help librarians succeed in changing library environments and closing with words of wisdom from interviewees.

Let's sum up what this book has covered. We started with a discussion of why another environment might be a good choice for you, what that change could look like, and what other librarians' views and experiences have been. Then we moved to various approaches for exploring opportunities, whether you're ready to move on or not. The chapter on CVs, résumés, and interviewing will help you get yourself in tip top shape when you're ready to move on. Changing jobs is stressful, so the next several chapters offered tools to strengthen your support systems, both internal and external. Then we looked at extending your professional reach via publishing, presenting, service, and similar activities. Through it all, we've woven quotes from our interviewees, and thoughts and experiences from both of us, in the hopes of giving you something personal and relatable. Most chapters end with questions for reflection that give you ways to probe deeper and connect what we've discussed back to your own situation. You can also use these as points of discussion with a mentor or other colleagues.

We hope you're feeling excited about the possibilities ahead of you. There are so many aspects and avenues of librarianship, we hope you are feeling inspired to pursue what is meaningful to you. We'll conclude with thoughts about the present and the future of libraries, and more insights and encouragement from our interviewees.

Current state of libraries

It's a challenging but also exciting time to be a librarian, and full of opportunities. There are so many people who need libraries, and so many librarians are seeing the work they do change peoples' lives in real, tangible ways. These are a few areas that seem especially relevant to the current state of libraries:

- Political challenges in the United States: There have been a few bills introduced recently specifically targeting librarians (Flood, 2020). These bills, sometimes threatening librarians with imprisonment, are aimed at what the politicians are calling "inappropriate material." But, of course, as all librarians know, what is inappropriate in one patron's eyes is a much-needed resource in another's. Though these bills have all seemed to fizzle out and not become law, they may have achieved their intended effect of intimidating librarians already.
- Library budgets wholly dependent upon governments/state structures: There has always been a level of politics involved in library budgets, and libraries are constantly fighting off budget cuts. In the US, there have recently been calls from politicians to eliminate funding for the IMLS (Institute of Museum and Library Services, 2020). The United Kingdom has had struggles with public library funding, but a recent report suggests that there might be a reprieve coming (Miller, 2019).
- High demand of libraries: Though budgets may not be large, libraries are still figuring out ways to serve their communities. In June 2019, the IMLS released their report on the 2016 Public Libraries of the United States Survey. In that report, they noted that there were over 1 billion library visits that year, and an increase of half a million programs over 2015's numbers (Institute of Museum and Library Services, 2019).
- Libraries having to reinvent themselves to offer nontraditional items and services: Perhaps out of a need to prove ROI (return on investment) to library funders, or perhaps just a result of evolving with their community, libraries have been embracing new technology and thinking of new things to lend to their patrons. Countless articles have been written on libraries lending baking pans and other equipment (Grillo, 2019), setting up makerspaces (American Library Association, 2016), and creating recording studios for anyone in the community to use.

- Libraries, and particularly scholarly communications librarians, are getting more and more involved in helping steer scholars toward open access journals to publish their research. As Open Access continues to grow, libraries find themselves at the forefront of promoting access to all, as well as grappling with the ongoing discussion around journal funding and subscription models. Libraries, patrons, and researchers in developed and developing countries are impacted in different ways.
- Poverty, homelessness, mental health issues, and related challenges. Many library patrons are facing difficult challenges in their lives. The libraries those patrons use often feel the impact, too, as they try to respond and help as possible. However, the need is tremendous and library resources are often already stretched thin. (Libraries, 2019) (Zulkey, 2019)

A note on COVID-19

As the authors complete the writing of this book, the COVID-19 pandemic is in full swing. Library buildings in affected countries are generally closed, according to the news reports we're hearing and some Googling of websites. When possible, staff members work remotely, doing any jobs that can be handled from off-site, typically from home. Some staff continue to work within the buildings, whether because they are considered "essential" or because their work can't be done remotely. Some library staff are unable to work remotely because they lack home internet or appropriate devices, or because the library building is closed to all.

Patrons can't access the libraries' physical resources because of concerns about spreading the virus but they have access to more online resources than ever. In addition to what libraries already provided, many publishers and vendors are making additional content available to support online learners (and to gain or retain a good impression from their customers) not to mention the availability of Open Access resources. Of course, some patrons, like some library staff, lack home internet and/or devices sufficient to provide access to this bounty.

The toll in human lives is as-yet unknown. The toll in numerous other dimensions is, too. A few thoughts about the future, from your authors writing from the midst of a pandemic, are below.

As the closures continue from weeks to months, librarians may face lay-offs or furloughs. It's unknown how long this will go on; how many will be forced to take other jobs – possibly outside the library field – in order to survive; and how many will retire (whether by choice or not). Some of our colleagues will die from the virus. Surely many already have around the world.

When library patrons can emerge from self-isolation and social distancing, will they be ready to gather at the library again? Some will be hungry for human interaction. Others may be leery of public gatherings for a long time. How long will it take before it seems normal again to be surrounded by a roomful of people attending a story time, library instruction session, or book group? When will librarians again gather for in-person department meetings and coffee, tea, or lunch breaks?

What will it take for patrons to feel comfortable borrowing library materials that countless people might have handled? What will it take to protect library staff who need to charge, return, shelve, and otherwise handle those same materials? Both physical protections and balm for frayed nerves will surely be needed.

As businesses shut down, unemployment rises, and tax revenues fall. Government coffers are being strained by increased demand and decreased income. Funding for libraries will likely decrease whether their funding agency is a government or private institution. Financial donations will likely decrease, too. Donations of materials may increase greatly however, as patrons stuck at home take to clearing out their unwanted stuff.

What will libraries take forward from the experience of doing so much more online? Will remote work become available for those who weren't permitted to do so before? What processes have been streamlined because they had to be? The authors' own library recently moved two previously paper-bound workflows online because it had to due to multiple departments working from home. We've learned that we can accomplish these things via email; will we go back?

Will patrons expect remote activities to continue? Maybe that online book group continues in addition to an in-person one. Like telemedicine, online activities are appealing to those who have a hard time getting out, whether due to infirmity, logistics, small children, etc. Surely, libraries will want to remain in that market.

The future of libraries

What is in store for the field of librarianship? As the saying goes, it feels like the only constant is change. Staying on top of trends and forecasts can help you adjust your professional development plans and career goals to focus on avenues that are likely to stay in demand.

At the beginning of Chapter 2 Exploring New Opportunities, we suggest a few websites you can visit to explore predictions and discussions of library trends. They're good venues to hear what innovative people have been doing. We wouldn't presume to put ourselves in that league, but we have shared below our thoughts on where the library field is headed, as well as some questions for reflection:

- Library funding will likely continue to be targeted for reduction. Library budget woes wax and wane with the economy and the predilections of the budgeting authorities at whatever levels affect your institution; it's part of the library landscape.
    - Knowing that you're unlikely to consistently get enough money for all the programs you want to run, all the materials you want to purchase,

and all the positions you want to fund, what actions can you take now to prepare for difficult and better times? What are your library's priorities, department by department? What must be funded, whether due to the demands of accreditation, funding requirements, or other external factors? If your budget is cut, what can you scale back or eliminate – and can you do it in such a way that the program can be reinstated efficiently in better times? If you faced a hiring freeze or early retirement offers, how could staffing shortages be managed? This is the time for creative solutions.
- On the flip side, if your library were to get a budget increase or an infusion of one-time funds, what's the most advantageous use that it could be put to? Is it possible to make a purchase that would reduce ongoing costs? Going back to your list of priorities, what is the biggest need?
- Let's do what we can to help ourselves: see what avenues are available to you to get involved in advocacy with your administration and with government at all levels. The trend of libraries needing to prove their value and to quantify that value (such as the academic trend of associating library funding with improved student success metrics) is and will continue to be a growing trend. How can your library prove its value?
- It seems likely that professional library organizations will continue to reorganize themselves. Some subdivisions or organizations may disappear, and some may combine with others. As new fields emerge and rise to prominence, new divisions or organizations may appear on the scene. Is there an aspect of library work that you feel is not currently well supported by a professional organization? If so, is there an existing organization you could fold this area into? If no existing organization is a good fit, at what level would a new professional organization need to be to adequately support this area – local, national, or international?
- Professional development costs may continue to shift to librarians, rather than libraries. While every library is different, it seems many never really recovered from the last economic downturn, and library budgets are never certain. If the industry norm becomes librarians shouldering the costs of travel, it may be difficult to get libraries to take those costs back. If your travel and professional development isn't covered by a library, how will you ensure you stay up-to-date in your librarianship?
  - Related to the above, there is an increasing trend for conferences to offer online participation. Costs are lowered due to lack of travel and lower still if multiple people pay for group attendance. Librarians can also present online. What does this do to the social and network aspect of conferences? How could that be brought online? Would you prefer an in-person or online conference experience?

- New technologies and formats will continue to enter the market, shifting how and what libraries will provide to patrons. Librarians will continue to push back on DRM issues and publisher restrictions and will need to look for creative solutions. What changes would you like to see in how your library provides resources? Do you see a shift toward perpetual ownership of digital materials? What are your patrons asking for that you don't currently provide?
- It becomes increasingly necessary for libraries to house other types of resources. In public libraries that could be post office or other package delivery and drop-off services; in academic libraries that could mean student support offices, tutoring, writing centers, or other student services. How would this type of merger affect how you provide services? What outreach opportunities do you see if such a merge were to happen? Are there services that you would like to see incorporated in the library space or partners in a shared building?
- Patron privacy will likely continue to be a big issue, with database providers potentially collecting more and more information digitally in the background (2018 top trends, 2018). There is definite potential for patrons, both at public and academic libraries, to be required to swipe an identification card, such as government- or school-issued ID or identify themselves in order to enter the library. There has been a major trend toward this on academic campuses, but some public libraries have been doing this to allow patrons access after-hours or early in the mornings. It is very likely that local police departments or governments will want to employ facial recognition software in public libraries at some point, perhaps even in academic libraries. Do you think patron privacy issues are being taken seriously in your library now? How do you see this changing in the future?
- As the ILS software improves, more avenues for libraries to share resources or work together will open up. If a librarian can easily integrate another library's ILS holdings into their workflow, it will make projects like shared acquisitions much, much easier. Improvements to the ILS should make things easier on the user side as well, allowing patrons to easily view library holdings, from all libraries they have access to, in their internet searches and shopping. What changes would you like to see to your ILS? Do you see your library working closely with another, perhaps even of a different library type?

Find your support

There are many ways to get personal support, both in person and online. Your friends already care about you, so be attentive to strengthening your friendships, especially if you're moving away geographically. Reach out to people who have made a similar transition and ask them questions about what you're getting yourself into. Don't be afraid to ask a lot of questions at all stages of your transition.

Don't neglect yourself

Pay attention to how you're feeling as you go through this process, particularly if you're relocating to a new area. You may have some emotional ups and downs, but that's all perfectly normal, and not indicative of a mistake. Cut yourself some slack and acknowledge that there will be a lot that you don't know initially. Give yourself time to learn.

Start connecting with the people you've asked to be your mentors and talk to them about their experiences. Check in with yourself and be honest about how you're feeling. If you are feeling stressed, or anxious, don't hold it all in. Take care of yourself as you enter this period of transition.

Push yourself out of your comfort zone

Once you're in a new position, you'll have opportunities that you didn't have before. Don't settle into your same old routine, and don't try to force your new job into the shape of your old job. Think about skills or experiences that have intrigued you and try to find a place for them in your new position. Don't be afraid to share your projects and expertise at conferences, on listservs, and in publications. Everyone making a name for themselves in this profession had a first paper, first presentation, or first committee post on their way to the top. You do not have to be perfect; you only need to move along the path.

Characteristics that may help you succeed

We asked our interviewees what personal characteristics helped people be successful at making a big transition within the library world. Though there was some overlap, we got a lot of different answers:

Willingness to ask questions

Maureen:

> Sometimes you think, well, I don't want to look like I don't know what I'm doing, but if you haven't worked in that type of system before, you need to ask those questions and not just assume that things are the same as what you've experienced with other organizations in other types of libraries.

Anna:

> The people I know who have successfully transitioned are those who are not afraid to say I don't know, they're not afraid to look a bit silly if they have to, and ask those dumb questions.

Willingness to talk to people and make connections

Lisa:

> I think it's about making connections, too, before [transitioning]. Nobody knows exactly when they're going to shift careers, right? But a lot of times people get stuck in their silo, and maybe someone who makes an effort to get involved with the local associations, regardless of what library sector they're for, and who gets involved with those social things that happen, however that happens, in a city or through networking at a conference. Someone who can leverage those kinds of connections as well, is useful. Because that's one of those things that can help the hiring committee look past the places you've worked is if they know who you are and they know what your skills are ... I hate to say those things, because it scares new people, but it's really important to get to know the people in your local industry. And it's really important not to just hang out with the people you work with. It's really important to meet people around. Because we have a lot to teach each other, too.

A true passion for librarianship

Audrey:

> I think characteristics that set great librarians apart from perfectly good librarians is that passion and the desire to help people ... I think it matters how you go into it. I consider it a sacred vocation, it is a calling rather than a job. And I think the people who treat it such, who believe that it's a really important job are going to do better than those who are there for a paycheck ... that attitude and internalizing it and making it really important to you if it wasn't already, I think that's what makes the best librarians. Not that you can't be one without that passion, but I think it's important.

Inventiveness

Brian:

> I think I would call it a kind of inventiveness. Can you take something that's on your CV or on your résumé, and can you look at something on their website or whoever it is you're interviewing with, and can you say, well what I'm doing here is similar to what they're asking for here? A lot of people can't do that.

Advocating for yourself

Diane:

> You definitely have to stand up for yourself. Advocate for yourself, because sometimes there's nobody else there that does it or understands what you do.

Flexibility

Kat:

> I think if you're not flexible it could be difficult.

Jodie:

> You need to be flexible, for sure. Willing to, very open to change. Open to hearing differences in opinion.

Enthusiasm and creativity

Marian:

> In my experience, people that are enthusiastic. People who just love the work who are passionate about the work. People who have, I'm going to say creativity, is the word I'm going to use, that doesn't mean they're necessarily artistic or able to create in the way an artist does, but people who generate lots of ideas and are willing to experiment and try.

Jenn:

> So it's just that willingness to jump in with both feet and be a jack of all trades. And that's probably the biggest trait that's different between the two, for me. So a good attitude and I don't know about bravery, but certainly a willingness to give it a shot.

Knowing yourself and your limits

Kady:

> You have to know yourself. I think for library size, it's sort of … coming to peace with your sphere of control, and what you have control over … So knowing yourself and knowing, oh can I deal with that or do I need to be more in control of my schedule and picking jobs that work for you in that way I think is useful. And then knowing yourself and how are you

with learning new systems. Do you need a lot of guidance or can you really jump in and do it on your own? ... So I think it's knowing yourself enough to say I am able to wait and be patient while the wheels of bureaucracy move. Working in a smaller library means you might be pulled in a lot of different directions, but you probably get to change things a lot faster and get things, see a need and meet it quicker than you would be able to in a larger system. So, I think it's, as with all career sort of things, it's knowing yourself and knowing your strengths and weaknesses and what you have a tolerance level for and don't.

Willingness to learn

Pam:

You've got people who just think either I'm going to absorb and move into this new environment or I'm going to resist and fight, or I'm going to leave. You've got different reactions to something coming in which is so different from what you've done before. So, it just kind of shows the different ways people react to either a change in their own workplace, or a different workplace. You either resist or you absorb, and you learn, and you develop and expand ... So, you've got to be very accommodating and very willing to learn new things and to recognize you can't be experts at everything.

Time management

Ronit:

When you're starting a new job, they don't just put the old, they don't just put the job on hold for you to learn it. So that's always, it's always tough to continue working while also learning the job, and so it's important to manage your time wisely in terms of knowing when to read up on things and when to get training sessions in and then balance it with actually getting the work done to meet the deadlines that are required.

Sense of humor

Yolanda:

You have to laugh your way through everything. So, at everything you do you've got to have a sense of humor. A sense of humor will help with any transition ... So, you have to laugh about everything as much as you can. A sense of humor and some perseverance would be helpful in any kind of transition that you're going to make.

Curiosity

Kathy:

> I think that curiosity and wanting to learn more about the place you're at. Whether that's moving into a public library and wanting to know more about the town, or moving into an academic library and wanting to know more about the campus and what's important on campus and what's going on on campus, I think those kinds of things can really help somebody make a transition.

Final words of wisdom

We'll leave you with some words of advice and inspiration from our interviewees:

Andy:

> The last few years have shown that no part of the profession is immune to change, and this has helped develop more support between the various parts of the profession. There's a great recognition that wherever you work, the same core skills are required, the challenges aren't that different, and that at the end of the day we need to work together in the face of concerted efforts to label library services as obsolete and unnecessary. This makes it easier to transfer from one area to another … The feeling I get is that whatever area you work in, the core skills are the same, and transferring is much easier.

Anna:

> I would always say do it, though, because I think actually, if you're good at your job, you'll be good at your job in whatever sector. And it might take a while to move between them, and it might take a while to get back if you decide you've made a mistake, but it won't be forever. We've got long, long, long working lives ahead of us … Why not take the chance? Nothing's going to go wrong that can't be undone.

Audrey:

> I would say, consider what your new atmosphere would look like, and if it seems like it would be rewarding for you, try it. You can always find another job somewhere else. It takes a long time. But if you think something is going to make you grow and fit well with you, then it is worth doing, and it's not going to be perfect right away.

Brian:

> Sometimes it feels really tough, and that you're never going to pull it off. But if you're persistent enough, you can do it ... There were a number of times over the last year that I was just like, "oh my god, I'm never going to get this, this is never going to happen" ... But it can happen, and it will happen.

Deb:

> We have a lot to learn from each other. I don't think we do that enough, and I don't think we take advantage enough of the expertise that our colleagues in other areas of librarianship have.

Fred:

> You shouldn't be afraid to look at another type of library ... It depends on what you're looking for. If you're trying to move up in one type of library, or if you want to get a broader view of the profession, which is not only in libraries anymore, it's many other places.

Jenn:

> I would definitely suggest taking that step outside your comfort zone. Moving across provinces was probably the best choice I made career-wise ... It is possible to change. I think that's the short version of all of this. It might not be the easier thing you've ever done, and it certainly might not be the most logical process for you to do it, but it's absolutely possible to make the change. The small town, big town, a library's a library.

Kady:

> Switching and trying something new is certainly one of the most rewarding decisions that I've made ... If you're thinking of doing it, that's probably a good indication that you should.

Kat:

> Be open to whatever opportunities might happen ... you have to be flexible and just be ready for whatever opportunity might be there.

Yolanda:

> Don't think about it too hard, just do it. Just transition. If it's something you're thinking about doing anyway, why not, just do it. Because

it's library world. It's not going to bring about the end of the world. And for the most part it's not going to harm you as a person. If it works out, great, you found this great new piece in a new part of the, a new piece and a new part of library world and you're enjoying it. Or you might find out it sucked, and this is just wrong. Well that's ok, you had a different experience that's going to impact what you do next and it's added something, no matter how horrible it may have seemed, it added something to your toolkit, or your toolbelt. So just do it, don't think too hard about it, it's library world. The world's not going to come to an end. If anything, we may save the world as librarians.

Stewart:

It's not necessarily something that people have to do, but I did find it beneficial. And that the perspective that you gain from seeing the same sorts of questions come up in all different work environments and all different types, the libraries have more in common with each other than differences. And that's the one thing to keep in mind. That there's far, far more commonality from one library to the next regardless of size, of the facility size or the collection, nature of the collection in terms of subject matter or format and so forth. There's far, far more similarities and far more is the same than is going to be different, so really the devil is in the details of what those differences are.

References

2018 Top Trends in Academic Libraries. (2018). *College & Research Libraries News*, 79(6), 286. https://doi.org/10.5860/crln.79.6.286

American Library Association (2016, June 13). Makerspaces. www.ala.org/pla/resources/tools/technology/makerspaces

Flood, A. (2020, January 16). Missouri Could Jail Librarians For Lending 'Age-Inappropriate' Books. *The Guardian*. www.theguardian.com/books/2020/jan/16/missouri-could-jail-librarians-for-lending-age-inappropriate-books-parental-oversight-of-public-libraries-bill

Grillo, E. (2019, September 16). Baking isn't Hard When You've Got a Library Card. Eater.com. www.eater.com/2019/9/16/20861011/public-library-cake-pans-on-loan-baking

Institute of Museum and Library Services (2019, June 5). In One Year, People Visited Public Libraries More Than a Billion Times. www.imls.gov/news/one-year-people-visited-public-libraries-more-billion-times

Institute of Museum and Library Services (2020, February 10). IMLS Statement on the President's FY 2021 Budget Proposal. www.imls.gov/news/imls-statement-presidents-fy-2021-budget-proposal

Libraries Respond: Services to Poor and Homeless People. (2019, August 19). American Library Association. www.ala.org/advocacy/diversity/librariesrespond/services-poor-homeless

Miller, R. (2019, December 2). UK Libraries Looking Up. *Library Journal*. www.libraryjournal.com/?detailStory=UK-Libraries-Looking-Up-Editorial

Zulkey, C. (2019, June 3). Give Them Shelter? *American Libraries*.

Further reading

Allard, S. (2018). Foundations and Futures. *Library Journal*, 143(17), 16–21.

Allard, S. (2019). The Analytics Age: UX Analysis Hits the Mainstream, LIS Graduates' Job Prospects Continue to Improve, and the Gender Salary Gap Narrows. *Library Journal*, 144(9), 32.

American Library Association. (2019). State of America's Libraries 2019. www.ala.org/news/state-americas-libraries-report-2019/

CILIP, The Library and Information Association. (viewed 2020 April 6) Current Issues. www.cilip.org.uk/page/CurrentIssues

CILIP, The Library and Information Association. (2018 October). Public libraries: the case for support. https://d3n8a8pro7vhmx.cloudfront.net/librariesdeliver/pages/76/attachments/original/1571054196/Public_Libraries_-_The_Case_for_Support_%28CILIP__The_Big_Issue%29.pdf

Evans, G., & Schonfeld, R. C. (2020, January 23). It's Not What Libraries Hold; It's Who Libraries Serve: Seeking a User-Centered Future for Academic Libraries. https://doi.org/10.18665/sr.312608

Hawkins, P. (2019). Change in Libraries: Directions for the Future, *Public Library Quarterly*, 38:4, 388–409, https://dx.doi.org/10.1080/01616846.2019.1595314

IFLA Annual Report 2018 (2018) www.ifla.org/node/92279

Kozubaev, S., & DiSalvo Ph.D., C. (2020). The Future of Public Libraries as Convivial Spaces: A Design Fiction. Conference on Supporting Group Work, 83. https://dl.acm.org/doi/10.1145/3323994.3369901

Appendix A: Survey on librarian career path and attitudes

The following is the survey on librarianship career paths and attitudes that the authors sent out in July 2019:
Questions and multiple-choice responses:

What type(s) of library have you worked for? Please select all that apply.
- Public library
- Academic library (two-year)
- Academic library (four-year and/or graduate)
- K-12 school
- Government
- Corporate
- Other (followed by free text box).

Do you think there is a bias in the library profession against hiring a librarian from a different library type?
- Yes
- No.

Has your current library hired a librarian from a different library type in the past five years? For example, if you are at a public library, have you hired a librarian coming from an academic library?
- Yes
- No
- Not sure.

Do you think librarians' skills transfer easily between library types?
- Yes
- No
- It depends (followed by free text box).

Appendix A

Do you think librarians should be open to moving across library types in the course of their career?
- Yes, it's often a good career move.
- Yes, but they should be careful.
- Maybe, it depends on the circumstances.
- No, it's rare for librarians to be successful in such a transition.
- No, it's a bad idea.

A link to the survey, created in Qualtrics, was posted to the following email lists and discussion platforms:
- ALA (American Library Association) Connect platform
- Auto-cat (authorities and cataloging email list)
- ERIL (electronic resources in libraries email list)
- Florida Library Association email list
- JISCmail email discussion list for the UK education and research communities
- Libraries Australia email list
- New Zealand Libraries email list
- OCLC Cataloging email list
- RUSA (Reference & User Services) Association email list
- Public Library Association Connect platform
- Special Library Association Connect "Open Forum."

Survey response totals:

The survey question about whether librarians' skills transfer easily between types had the option "it depends" followed by a free-text box where respondents could type their input. All of those comments ran to more than 25 pages in total, so we are unable to share them all here. A sample is included in Chapter 1 and a fuller sample is included below:

- We've seen public librarians have a difficult time making the shift to a tenure track mindset.
- On the type of position one is transferring to.
- I think it really depends on their job duties and experience. In some big pictures ways (i.e., project management), yes they transfer easily enough. Technical skills and a general understanding of the landscape of another library type can be very challenging.
- Informed more by functional rather than sectoral specialisms.
- There are differences in cataloging and public services between public and academic.
- Personality and openness to new learning experiences play a pivotal role.
- On whether the type and volume of work is similar.
- Public, academic and corporate institutions all have quirks. The base skills may transfer but the work environments are very different.
- On the position.

Table A1 Survey responses

Type of library worked in	Total respondents	No bias against hiring a librarian from a different library type	Yes, bias against hiring a librarian from a different library type	No, skills don't transfer easily	Yes, skills transfer easily	It depends (skill transfer)
Only academic library (two-year)	25	12	13	2	11	12
Only academic library (four-year and/or graduate)	313	95	218	15	144	154
Only corporate	20	8	12	0	12	8
Only government	29	16	13	1	17	11
Only K-12 school	161	69	92	6	94	61
Other	47	21	26	2	26	19
Only public library	243	100	143	12	119	112
Worked in more than one type	909	372	533	23	528	354

Table A2 Survey responses

Type of library worked in	Total respondents	No, bad idea (moving across type)	No, success is rare (moving across type)	Maybe (open to moving across type)	Yes, be careful (should be open to moving across type)	Yes often good (moving type)	No (current library hired from other type)	Yes (current library hired from other type)	Not sure (current library hired from other type)
Academic library (two-year)	25	0	0	10	3	12	6	15	4
Academic library (four-year and/or graduate)	313	1	0	128	62	122	91	158	64
Corporate	20	0	0	7	1	12	12	5	3
Government	29	0	1	7	6	15	8	18	3
K-12 school	161	1	1	67	17	75	112	31	18
Other	47	0	1	14	7	25	22	21	4
Public library	243	0	1	83	35	124	54	141	48
Worked in more than one type	909	0	1	232	122	550	213	532	160

- Not as easily I expected after trying to move to academic libraries after a career in specialist libraries.
- I started out in a branch of a public library in a large city that served mainly immigrants. It was in 1992, when the internet was just coming in. I then was able to transfer to the business library within the same public library system and worked part time in academic libraries before landing a full time position at my current place 20 years ago. The answers in the public system were mainly quick answers as opposed to more lengthy inquiries in the academic setting. All users need some help ... some are better at asking their questions and others know that the data they need is costly. When I tried to find a job in the corporate world, at the entry level, 20+ years ago, recruiters said it would be difficult to make the transition from one to another. I think there are fewer opportunities in the corporate world for work and for entry level positions. I stayed at the public library for six years, five at the business library and I needed to grow.
- Some library types have more individuals of one skill type over others. For example, I think public libraries are less likely to promote skills helpful in negotiating contracts with academic database providers.
- On the staff size and complexity of resource environment of the library.
- I think it depends on the librarian that is moving and whether or not they are quick to adapt their skills.
- If the system and the structure permits innovation.
- I think it's more about the size of the library than the type of library.
- Different classification types/patron needs.
- Depends on the position: circ [circulation] coordinators and catalogers are pretty universal, but research librarianship isn't.
- There's definitely a learning curve between style of information instruction/guidance, but as long as one is adaptable it should run relatively smoothly.
- Assuming that the academic librarian is a liaison or reference worker, yes it transfers nicely. If it is a research based library or if the librarian is required to teach, it can be a little rough.
- Having worked in several academic libraries and with many public ones, both tech and public services have different focuses/tools.
- Basically, yes but university type of cataloging is much different than public library cataloging.
- Depends on what their previous role was and what their new role will be.
- The basic knowledge is the same. If the transitioning librarian is given adequate training, I believe they can be successful working in a new type of library.
- Public-facing is similar, research doesn't cross over well, technology crosses a bit.
- On the librarian's initiative and ability to effectively map skills across different job duties.

- I do not have any experience to judge this question. Some areas are surely easier than others, however (for example, academic libraries obviously need more in-depth research skills).
- It's harder for technical services librarians' skills to transfer from academic to public libraries.
- From most libraries yes, but not all persons ... depends on the departments they worked in.
- On work experience and skillset. Public service/acquisitions are easily transferable.
- In my experience, the skills are job specific and not library type specific.
- Much of this depends on the audience that a librarian supports. If the audience changes dramatically from one job to the next, then the adjustment might be extended.
- It could be about a persona, or also about needs in terms of liaison area and the amount of time onboarding/adjustment would take.
- General skills are transferable, subject-specific not as easily transferred.
- Depends on the role: how much front-facing vs. behind the scenes experience, skills with specific populations/ages.
- Some skills transfer well. Some areas of librarianship (reference comes to mind) require a lot of learning to move between library types.
- It depends on the skills involved, the duties of the job(s), efficacy in deploying the skills, and the willingness of management to allow librarians to adapt/transfer skills.

Appendix B: Example résumé and CV

Following are Tina's 2018 CV and then her 2015 résumé. Comparing the two may help if you are drafting "the other" document from the one you have, or if you are new to creating either type. These documents, especially the CV, have been edited for space and clarity, providing examples but reducing length.

Tina Herman Buck

Electronic Resources Librarian

Very Large University

EDUCATION

City University (City, State)

- Master of Library Science (MLS), YYYY
- Bachelor of Arts, YYYY

PROFESSIONAL EXPERIENCE

Electronic Resources Librarian
Very Large University (city, state)
MMYYYY – present

Acquisitions & Metadata Librarian
Small University (city, state)
MMYYYY – MMYYYY

Cataloger
Big City Public Library (city, state)
MMYYYY – MMYYYY

138   *Appendix B*

Senior Serials Collection Librarian
Big County Library System (city, state)
MMYYYY – MMYYYY

Technical Services Supervisor
Multi-type Cooperative (city, state)
MMYYYY – MMYYYY

Assistant Head of Technical Services
Medium City Library (city, state)
MMYYYY – MMYYYY

Head of Technical Services
Small Town Public Library (city, state)
MMYYYY – MMYYYY

PERFORMANCE OF PROFESSIONAL RESPONSIBILITIES

Electronic Resources Librarian, Very Large University (city, state)

Associate Librarian MMYYYY –
Assistant Librarian MMYYYY – MMYYYY

- **Continuing Resources (Serials and Databases)**
  - Major duties
    - Co-led migration to new knowledge base, journals a–z list, and link-resolver product from vendor Z.
    - Maintain and enhance database access points in database a-z list and in ILS. Maintain electronic serials records in ILS.
    - Manage the print serials unit whose responsibilities include print serials, standing orders, microforms, and projects to improve existing collection materials in those areas.
  - Major accomplishments
    - Increase accuracy and completeness of the knowledge base. Guide staff on training and learning relevant terminology.
    - Increased accuracy and usability of the database a–z list through a more visible search box, asset consolidation, and timely updates.
    - Led the print serials unit in improving the subscription renewal, resulting in heightened title control and elimination of undesirable formats.
    - With serials unit, implement alternatives to serials binding to reduce escalating binding costs.

Appendix B 139

- **Coordinate Electronic Resources Cataloging**
  - Major duties
    - Coordinate between Acquisitions & Collections and Cataloging Departments on matters related to electronic resources cataloging, such as new acquisitions, cancellations, MARC record sourcing, and entitlement questions.
  - Major accomplishments
    - Ensure that the primary Electronic Resources Cataloger is informed of purchases, new or cancelled subscriptions, and changes requiring bibliographic work. Created a shared file to log this information.
- **Co-led the Electronic Resources Team**
  - Major duties
    - Troubleshoot and resolve electronic resources problems for librarians and end users.
    - Maximize access, functionality, and user-friendly presentation.
    - Assist with acquisitions-related functions such as obtaining quotes and providing oversight of invoice payment and fiscal tracking.
  - Major accomplishments
    - Address questions, information requests, and problem reports as promptly and thoroughly as possible.
    - Use problem reports as a catalyst for broader quality assurance projects
- **ILS (Integrated Library System) Migration Project**
  - Major duties
    - Appointed to the Electronic Resource Management (ERM) Working Group for the ILS Migration Project.
  - Major accomplishments
    - Elected chair. Guided the group through learning the system and how the ERM related to the vendor knowledge bases and to other parts of the ILS. Lead a collaborative decision-making process to select data options and system settings. Performed multiple rounds of data and system functionality testing and reported problems and unexpected outcomes.
    - Served on the Statewide Implementation Team, meeting bi-weekly to share information and give input about migration-wide issues.
    - Served on the local Implementation Team, sharing information and planning implementation.

- Guided library serials and electronic resources staff through training, data-testing, and consideration of workflow changes.
- **Supervisor**
  - Supervise two direct reports.

Acquisitions & Metadata Librarian, Small University (city, state)
MMYYYY – MMYYYY

- Managed acquisitions, cataloging, authority control, and other Technical Services functions. Tracked and expended an annual budget of approximately $xxx,xxx. Created policies and procedures. Supervised Technical Services staff of one.
- Database maintenance and enhancement.
  - Cataloged using OCLC, ILS, and MARCedit. Applied knowledge of standards such as RDA, AACR2, MARC, Library of Congress Subject Headings, and Library of Congress and Dewey Decimal Classification schemes.
  - Managed and performed database maintenance and enhancement for bibliographic, authority, order, item, and holdings records.
  - Created load tables and batch-loaded vendors' MARC record sets for numerous e-book and streaming video platforms, including a large PDA (patron-driven acquisitions) program.
- Integrated Library System (ILS)
  - Extensive use of ILS for technical services functions. Managed ILS interactions with vendor services such as EDIFACT ordering and invoicing, and OCLC WorldCat Cataloging Services. Trained staff and served as a resource person.
  - Co-led implementation of ILS Electronic Resources Management module.
  - Chaired the ILS Migration Team in investigating next-gen ILS systems.
- Discovery Layers
  - Co-led implementation of the Vendor Z Discovery Layer. Collaborated on management of our installation.
- Public services and liaison.
  - Library liaison to the College of Sciences and Mathematics, including collection development, creation of LibGuides, instruction, and research assistance.
  - Provide research assistance in person, via phone, instant-message, and email.
- Interim Collection Management Librarian: MMYYYY – MMYYYY.

- Interim Serials & Electronic Resources Librarian: MMYYYY – MMYYYY.

Cataloger, Big City Public Library (city, state)

MMYYYY – MMYYYY

- Original and copy cataloging on videos in English and Spanish. Performed authority maintenance. Classify using Dewey Decimal Classification scheme.
- Member of the ILS Migration Team. Participated in department planning and data-testing for migration from ILS A to ILS B. Implemented the cataloging and related modules and instructed cataloging and public services staff. Created the cataloging manual for staff. Collaborated with reference and IT personnel in improving bibliographic display and search functionality in the OPAC.

Senior Serials Collection Librarian, Big County Library System (city, state)

MMYYYY – MMYYYY

- Collection management of serials and reference materials for county library system.
- Financial responsibility for more than $xxx,xxx for serials and reference materials.
- Led the newly created Reference and Continuations Unit.
- Developed and implemented a template of periodicals collections based on branch size and community demographics.
- Interim head of Interlibrary Loan. Led project to update ILL software.

Technical Services Supervisor, Multi-type Cooperative (city, state)

MMYYYY – MMYYYY

- Oversaw all aspects of Technical Services department, including 1–3 staff. Performed original and copy cataloging on OCLC.
- Technical Services consultant. Advised librarians and staff from 300 member libraries (academic, public, school, and special) regarding cataloging, acquisitions, retrospective conversion, and processing.
- Taught and/or coordinated Technical Services continuing education courses to member librarians and library staff.

- Used ILS from Vendor Y, Cataloging, Acquisitions, and online catalog modules. First library in consortia to implement Acquisitions; served as resource for other libraries.
- Co-managed State Systems Materials Purchasing Co-operative, according to state purchasing laws, seeking the best vendor discount and performance on most library materials for 600+ libraries of all types. Administered state-funded MARC Conversion Grants, which assisted libraries performing network-related MARC conversion.
- Wrote informative articles and book reviews for the quarterly newsletter.

Assistant Head of Technical Services, Medium City Library (city, state)

MMYYYY – MMYYYY

- Assisted Department Head in day-to-day administration and planning.
- Original and copy cataloging and classification, including Spanish language materials.
- Trained and served as resource person for four copy catalogers and one cataloger.
- Provided reference assistance at main library desk.

Head of Technical Services, Small Town Public Library (city, state)

MMYYYY – MMYYYY

- Copy-cataloged and classified all materials. Planned and implemented retrospective conversion of reference collections. Developed special handling of Spanish, Russian, and Vietnamese materials.
- Supervised four staff.
- Reference and Collection Development duties. Occasional supervision of circulation desk.

RESEARCH AND CREATIVE ACTIVITIES

PUBLICATIONS

Articles in Peer Reviewed Journals
- Buck, Tina Herman, and Sara K. Hills. "Diminishing Short-Term Loan Returns: A Four-Year View of the Impact of Demand-Driven Acquisitions on Collection Development at a Small Academic Library." *Library Resources & Technical Services,* 61, no. 1 (January 2017): 51–56.

Conference Paper Publications:
- Appleton, Betsy, Tina Herman Buck, and Carol Seiler, "Change It Up: Growing Your Career in a Wildly Different Organization." *Roll with the Times, or the Times Roll Over You: 2016 Proceedings of the Charleston Library Conference* (2017): 378–383. http://dx.doi.org/10.5703/1288284316475

PRESENTATIONS

National Conferences and Meetings
- Appleton, Betsy and Tina Herman Buck. "Size Does(n't) Matter: Growing Your Career in a Wildly Different Organization." Presentation at the Electronic Resources & Libraries (ER&L) Conference, Austin Texas, April 4, 2016.

Regional Conference
- Buck, Tina Herman and Sara K. Hills. "A DDA Program Four Years Later: Evaluation and Sustainability." Presentation at the AMIGOS Online Conference: E-Books in Libraries: An Update. November 16, 2015.

State Conference
- Buck, Tina Herman, Elizabeth Lightfoot, and Shelly Schmucker. "Unleash the ERM!" Presentation at the Florida Library Association Conference, Orlando, Florida, May 24, 2018

POSTER SESSIONS AT NATIONAL CONFERENCES

- Piascik, Jeanne, Kristine Shrauger, Lindsey Ritzert, Tina Buck, and Ying Zhang. "Two Barcodes, Many Headaches." Poster presented at the Innovative Users' Group Conference, National Harbor, MD, 2017. http://stars.library.ucf.edu/ucfscholar/79

PROFESSIONAL DEVELOPMENT

Attendance at professional conferences
- ER&L (Electronic Resources & Libraries), YYYY–
- State Library Association Conference, YYYY, YYYY–
- Vendor ILS Users Group Conference, YYYY, YYYY

Attendance at training sessions and workshops
- **Serials management:** Project Transfer, GOKb; EBSCOnet; Full Text Finder; Protect Your Patrons from Predatory Publishers
- **Electronic Resources Management, Discovery, and Statistics**: EBSCO Discovery Service, COUNTER (Counting Online Usage

of NeTworked Electronic Resources); The Practicality of Managing "E"
- **Cataloging**: RDA, BibFrame, and Linked Data

Current Professional Memberships
- American Library Association (ALA) YYYY–present
- State Library Association, YYYY–present

SERVICE

National
- ALCTS (Association for Library Collections & Technical Services) Continuing Resources Section, elected Member-At-Large, YYYY–YYYY.
- Vendor ILS Users Group Conference (VIUG)
  - Local Arrangements Committee, YYYY
  - Moderator at Load Profilers' Forum, YYYY

Conference Report
- Buck, Tina Herman. "CRS Standards Forum: 2017 Midwinter Meeting." *ALCTS News* (March 2017): www.ala.org/alctsnews/features/mw2017-crs-standards-forum

State
- Technical Services Standing Committee for the Cooperative, MMYYYY–MMYYYY.
- State Library Association, Automation and Technology Round Table
  - Alternate Councilor (YYYY)
  - Winner, YYYY conference stipend award

University (at VLU)
- Faculty Senator YYYY–YYYY

University (at Small University)
- Faculty Development Committee (a.k.a. Teaching Awards Committee), YYYY–YYYY.

Library (at VLU)
- Chair, Employee of the Year Selection Committee, YYYY

Library (at Small University)
- Chaired numerous search committees

Mentoring
- Mentor a library school student as part of the State University Information Science mentorship program, throughout her tenure until graduation, XXXX–XXXX

Community
- Non-university-related community organization:
  - President, YYYY–YYYY
  - Editor, weekly electronic newsletter, YYYY-

TINA HERMAN BUCK

[PERSONAL ADDRESS]
[PERSONAL PHONE NUMBER] | [PERSONAL EMAIL ADDRESS]

EXPERIENCE

ACQUISITIONS & METADATA LIBRARIAN, SMALL UNIVERSITY, (CITY, STATE)

MM/YYYY – present

- Manage acquisitions, cataloging, vendor relations, authority control, and other Technical Services functions. Track and expend an annual budget of approximately $xxx,xxx. Create policies and procedures.
- Catalog on OCLC and Integrated Library System. Apply knowledge of RDA (Resource Description and Access), AACR2, MARC, Library of Congress Subject Headings, and Library of Congress and Dewey Decimal classification.
- Manage and perform bibliographic database maintenance and enhancement. Batch-load vendors' MARC record sets for numerous e-book and streaming video platforms. Use Integrated Library System functions and MarcEdit to batch-update records.
- Supervise and train Technical Services staff of one.
- Extensive use of ILS for technical services functionality. Responsible for all load-profiling. Manage ILS interactions with vendor services such as EDIFACT ordering and invoicing, and OCLC WorldCat Cataloging services. With the ERM team, implemented ILS's ERM module. Also utilize serials, ERM, inventory, and circulation functions.

- With the Discovery Layer team, implemented the Vendor Z Discovery Layer. Collaborate on management of our installation.
- Chair the Integrated Library System Team in investigating next-gen ILS systems.
- Established and manage the first demand-driven acquisitions programs at the university library for e-books, streaming videos, and articles.
- Lead the Catalog Team to maximize public utility of our OPAC, prior to implementation of our discovery layer.
- Library liaison to the College of Sciences and Mathematics, including collection development, creation of LibGuides, and guidance to research students.
- Perform instruction sessions for general-education and natural-science research classes.
- Provide research assistance in person, and via phone, instant-message chat, and email.
- Chaired numerous search committees, most recently for the Collection Development Librarian and for the Electronic & Continuing Resources Librarian (both in 2014). Currently serving on search committee for Digital Services Manager.
- Interim Collection Development Librarian: MMYYYY – MMYYYY.
- Interim Electronic & Continuing Resources Librarian: MMYYYY – MMYYYY.
- University Service activities include:
  - Sponsor for Student Group, YYYY – present
  - Faculty Development Committee (a.k.a Teaching Awards Committee), YYYY-YYYY

Cataloger, Big City Public Library (City, State)

YYYY–YYYY

- Original and copy cataloging on videos, books, and audios in English and Spanish. Performed authority maintenance. Use Dewey Decimal Classification.
- Resource person for department staff regarding OCLC, ILS, and technical services procedures.
- Member of the ILS Migration Team. Participated in department planning and data-testing for migration. Implemented the cataloging and related modules, and instructed cataloging and public services staff. Created the cataloging manual for staff. Collaborated with reference and IT personnel in improving bibliographic display and search functionality in the new OPAC.

Senior Serials collection Librarian, Big County Library System (City, State)

YYYY–YYYY

- Collection management of serials and reference materials for large county library system.
- Financial responsibility for more than $xxx,xxx for serials and reference materials.
- Led the newly created Reference and Continuations Unit.
- With purchasing officer, developed the RFP governing periodical purchasing.
  The bid purchased 3000 subscriptions spanning 700 print titles.
- Developed and implemented a template of periodicals collections based on branch size and community demographics.
- Collaborated with collections, cataloging, and IT staff to update and complete serials cataloging and item data.
- Collaborate with branch reference staff on collection management projects, such as "opening day collections" for newly constructed branches and the evaluation and weeding of print reference materials.
- Cataloged standing orders on ILS and OCLC.
- Interim head of Interlibrary Loan.

Technical Services Supervisor, Multi-Type Cooperative (city, state)

YYYY–YYYY

- Oversee all aspects of Technical Services department, including supervision and training of 1–3 staff. Performed original and copy cataloging on OCLC. Classification in DDC.
- Resource specialist for Technical Services. Advise 300 member libraries (academic, public, school, and special) regarding cataloging, acquisitions, retrospective conversion, and processing.
- Teach and/or coordinate Technical Services-related continuing education courses to member librarians and library staff.
- Use ILS from Vendor Y for Cataloging, Acquisitions, and OPAC modules. First library in consortia to implement Acquisitions; served as resource for other libraries.
- Co-manage State Systems Materials Purchasing Co-operative, according to state purchasing laws, seeking the best vendor discount and performance on most library materials for 600+ libraries of all types.

- Administer state-funded MARC Conversion Grants: award and assist libraries performing network-related MARC conversion.
- Part of start-up team for StateCat, a statewide resource-sharing database. Serve on Executive, Implementation and Cataloging Committees. Perform original cataloging on OCLC, and database maintenance on ILS Vendor X Product, as the network cataloger for StateCat.

Assistant Head, Technical Services, Medium City Library (city/state)

YYYY–YYYY

- Assist Dept. Head in day-to-day administration and planning.
- Original and copy cataloging and classification, including Spanish language materials.
- Train and serve as resource person for four copy catalogers and one cataloger.
- Provide reference at main library desk.
- Provide Technical Services support to branch and main library staff.

Head of Technical Services, Small Town Public Library (city, state.)

YYYY–YYYY

- Catalog all materials.
- Supervise, train and direct workflow of four technicians.
- Increased technical services production by over 300%.
- Planned and implemented retrospective conversion of reference collections.
- Developed special processing of Spanish, Russian, and Vietnamese materials.
- Reference and Collection Development duties.
- Occasional supervision of Circulation desk.

PUBLICATIONS

- Ferris, Kady, and Tina Herman Buck. "An Ethos Of Access: How A Small Academic Library Transformed Its Collection-Building Processes." *Collection Management* 39.2/3 (2014): 127–144.

PROFESSIONAL ACTIVITIES

- Member, ALA
- Vendor ILS User's Group (VIUG)

- YYYY conference presentation: "Learning to Juggle: Big Batches of Records, Lots of Vendors, and the New World of Technical Services."
  - YYYY conferences presentation: "Create Lists: Let's Rev the Engine."
  - Served as recorder or moderator at Load Profilers' Forum for several years.
- State Library Association
  - YYYY conference presentation: "LibGuides: Content without Coding."
  - Automation and Technology Round Table
    - Alternate Councilor (YYYY-YYYY)
    - Conference Stipend Committee (multiple years)
    - Winner, YYYY conference stipend
- North American Serials Interest Group (NASIG)
  - YYYY conference presentation: "Collection Development in Public Libraries."
- Continuing education activities include:
  - Electronic Resources & Libraries Conference (ER&L) (multiple years);
  - State STEM (Science, Technology, Engineering, and Mathematics) Librarians Conference (multiple years);
  - Resource Description and Access (RDA) Gets Real in New Orleans: an ALCTS pre-conference (YYYY);
  - Vendor ILS training workshops: Acquisitions; Load Profiling; Systems Administration and Statistical Reporting; Advanced Systems Administration; and WebOPAC Administration (YYYY-YYYY)
  - Advanced Excel workshops;
  - Webinars about Resource Description and Access (RDA), Functional Requirements for Bibliographic Records (FRBR), Linked Data, BibFrame, and predatory open-access publishers, as well as numerous vendor meetings and training sessions for various products.

EDUCATION

- M.L.S. City University School of Library and Information Science, YYYY
- B.A. City University, YYYY

Index

Note: Page numbers in *italics* indicate figures and in **bold** indicate tables on the corresponding pages.

academic librarians 6–7, 13
ACRLog 112
"Addressing Psychosocial Factors with Library Mentoring" 71
adjustment process 92–100
advocacy, self- 125
Against the Grain Conferences, Meetings, and Webinars 106
age of mentors 71
ALA Connect 27
ALA Midwinter Conference 110
ambiguity 93–94
assumptions, dealing with 96
awards and honors 40

Barrett, L. F. 90
blogging 112

cataloging 4–5, 9
Charleston Conference on Library Acquisitions 106
Chronicle of Higher Education 99
Clance, P. R. 97–98
classes and events, library 10
collection development 8, 9, 10–11
community mentors 65–66
community outreach 8
conference mentors 64–65
conferences and presenting 105–110
consortia 10
continuing education 40
contract positions 14
coordinating departments 92
co-presenters for conference presentations 106–107
cover letters 41–48

COVID-19 117, 119–120
creativity 125
cross-training 28
culture, adjusting to new 96–97
culture shock 94–95, *95*
curiosity 127
curriculum vitae (CV) 34–35; awards and honors on 40; component parts of 36–48; customized for each job application 41; education listed on 36–37; example 137–149; professional activities and professional memberships on 40; professional development and training on 40; professional experience on 37; research and creative works or publications and presentations listed on 40; résumés compared to 35–36; service listed on 37–39
customization: of cover letters 43–48; of résumés/CVs for each job application 41

developing countries, libraries in 16–17

Electronic Resources & Libraries (ER&L) Conference 106
emotions management: in the adjustment process 92–100; dealing with nerves in 91–92; interviewee comments on and experiences with 100–101; introduction to 88–89; and knowing how you feel 90; related to stress and transitions 90
enthusiasm 125

Farrell, B. 71
flexibility 125
focus of new positions 77
formal versus informal mentoring 62
funding, research 105
future of libraries 120–122

Hasty, D. 106
"How to Overcome Impostor Syndrome" 99
humor 126

Imes, S. A. 97–98
impostor syndrome 71, 97–98; finding support for 99–100; recognizing 98–99
In the Library With the Lead Pipe 112
independent/single site libraries 10
informal mentorship 62
Information Today 106
institutional mentors 64
integrated library system (ILS) 3–4, 5, 77, 83, 122
interviews 48–55; assessing the experience of 54–55; benefits of multiple 53–54; comfort for disappointing 55; contextualizing your past work for your present situation for 52–53; interviewee comments on 57–58; laying the groundwork in preparing for 56–57; length of 49–50; personnel involved in 49; pre-interview screening materials for 50–51; preparing for, in different library environment 51–52; requiring a presentation 50; travel for 50
inventiveness 124
involvement/non-involvement 93
isolation 92–93, 119

James, J. M. 62
job applications: customizing cover letters for 43–48; customizing résumés/CVs for 41; as request for more information 55
job postings 26–27

Kashdan, T. B. 90

learning, willingness for 126
librarians: adjustment process for 92–100; on changing environments 20–23; characteristics of successful 123–127; cross-training by 28; example of transitioning 1–7; exploring the profession 25–27; final words of wisdom for 127–129; finding support 122; making the job your own 29–30; networking by 31–32; not neglecting self 123; professional associations for 30–31, 40, 121; professional development for 30–32, 40, 121; pushing outside their comfort zone 123; rank of 13; reasons for switching 7–8; survey of 18–20, 131–136, **133–134**; unusual options for 13–17; working on new initiatives 28–29; *see also* emotions management; new colleagues
libraries: academic 6–7, 13; classes and events offered by 10; collection models for 10–11; consortia or independent/single site or system 10; current state of 118–119; in developing countries 16–17; differences and similarities in types and sizes of 8–13; future of 120–122; impact of COVID-19 on 117, 119–120; learning about accomplishments of individual 82–83; librarian impressions of changing types of 18–20; misconceptions about 17–18; multi-type 14; organization of 82; patron focus of 9–10; philosophies about activities in 8–9; priorities of individual 78–79; public 5–6, 18; reports and statistics on 83; rural 14–15; services provided by 10; size of 11–12; structure of parent organization and reporting structure outside 12–13; temporary or contract positions in 14
Library Conference Planner 106
Library Journal 14
library vendors 13
life coach/fan 65
lightning rounds 110
long-term mentors 71

Master of Library Science (MLS) programs 2, 36
McKnight, P. E. 90
mentors: age of 71; becoming 70–72, 72; bubble chart of 72; community 65–66; conference 64–65; finding 68–69; formal versus informal 62; institutional 64; life coach or fan 65; other kinds of learning from

152   Index

colleagues and associates as 68; peer 66–67; professional/career 62–64; qualities of 70–71; reasons to be 61–62; self-mentorship and 67–68; short-term versus long-term 71; support group 66–67; two-way street of 71–72; types of 62–68
moderating of panel discussions 110
multi-type libraries 14
Musings about Librarianship 112

networking 31–32, 124
new colleagues: being aware of how often you mention how things were done in your old library 87; changing your assumptions and expectations 74–75; connecting to other parts of the organization outside the library 84–86; fighting new job brain fog 79–80; figuring out your library's priorities 78–79; focus of 77; learning about your library's accomplishments 82–83; learning your job 80–82; learning your library and institution 82; new coworkers of 83–84; in a new geographic area 86–87; organization of new library and 82; reports and statistics available to 83; resources available to 75–76; software and online tools for 77–78; *see also* librarians
new job brain fog 79–80

OCLC 3
outreach 8

panel discussions 110
para-professional 2
parent organization structure 12–13
passion for librarianship 124
past put in context 96
patron focus 9–10
PechaKucha 110
peer mentors 66–67
philosophies about library activities 8–9
poster sessions 109
pre-interview screening 50–51
presenting at conferences 105–110
privacy, patron 122
professional associations 30–31, 40, 121
professional development 30–32, 40, 121
professional experience on résumés/ curriculum vitae 37

professional/career mentors 62–64
Public Library Association (PLA) 106
public services librarians 5–6, 18
publishing 103–104, 111–112

question asking 123

racial microaggressions 71
rank in academic libraries 13
reading 27
reference services 5–6, 9
reporting structure 12–13
resources available to new colleagues 75–76
résumés 34–35; awards and honors on 40; compared to curriculum vitae (CV) 35–36; component parts of 36–48; customized for each job application 41; education listed on 36–37; example 137–149; professional activities and professional memberships on 40; professional development and training on 40; professional experience on 37; research and creative works or publications and presentations listed on 40; service listed on 37–39
Revuluri, S. 99
rural libraries 14–15

scholarly articles 111–112
Scholarly Kitchen 112
scholarship: conference presentations on 105–110; finding a topic for 112–113; importance of 113–114; interviewees' perspectives on 114–115; introduction to 103–104; research and 104–105; writing and publishing 111–112
Schwartz, M. 14
self-advocacy 125
self-awareness 125–126
self-mentorship 67–68
sense of humor 126
Serials Librarian, The 27
Serials Review 27
service listed on résumés/curriculum vitae 37–39
short-term mentors 71
size of libraries 11–12
small libraries 17
stage fright 107–108
stress and transitions 90

supervisory experience 26–27
support groups 66–67

technical services librarians 4–5
temporary positions 14
time management 126
Toronto Public Library 112

U curve 94–95, *95*

vendors, library 13
volunteer opportunities at conferences 109–110

Wayback Machine 56
weeding and collection development policy 8
writing and publishing 111–112

For Product Safety Concerns and Information please contact our EU
representative GPSR@taylorandfrancis.com
Taylor & Francis Verlag GmbH, Kaufingerstraße 24, 80331 München, Germany

www.ingramcontent.com/pod-product-compliance
Lightning Source LLC
Chambersburg PA
CBHW061350300426
44116CB00011B/2062